MY STRANGEST CASE

A CRIME CLUB SELECTION

EIGHTEEN law-enforcement officers from all over the world have contributed to this exciting collection—each man recounting the strangest case of his career. The stories vary from the account of the suave, sophisticated cat burglar of Honolulu to the case of the Australian Bluebeard whose nine wives became his victims, and the telepathic police aide in Vancouver who could read the minds of his criminals.

Ex-Chief Superintendent Frederick Cherrill of Scotland Yard and J. Edgar Hoover are two of the distinguished contributors to this unusual nonfiction anthology.

Scene: Around the world.

The material in this book has appeared previously as a part of the Reuters Features Syndicate.

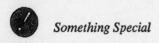 *Something Special*

MY
STRANGEST
CASE

by Police Chiefs of the World
Edited by Kurt Singer

Published for the *Crime Club* by
Doubleday & Company, Inc., Garden City, New York 1958

Contents

Introduction

Crime and espionage are closely related. As a former intelligence officer I have found my way into the labyrinth of murder in many foreign lands. From the spy webs of international intrigue to the spider webs of crime are only a few steps.

I have shined so many blue gabardine suits on the unupholstered police benches of the world that now I feel it is time for the police chiefs to tell their own tales.

Every story in this book is authentic in its source and presentation, and nowhere has exaggeration or pretense been allowed to take over from truth.

Police regulations differ according to the country, and not every police chief is at liberty to sign his name to a personal account of his "strangest case." Hence, to comply with official decree, it has been necessary to substitute a pseudonym in the stories from Moscow, Marseilles, San Francisco, Trinidad, and Vienna. This is the only deviation in the factual presentation of the material on which this book is based.

Buena Park, California   KURT SINGER
1958

MY STRANGEST CASE

Two Minutes to Eternity

by Police Reporter David Broderick, Retired
Sheriff, Marin County, California, U.S.A.

THE MORNING I went to see Burton Abbott die in the gas chamber at San Quentin was cold and blustery and the sharp winds that swept San Francisco from the Golden Gate and the broad Pacific beyond had not yet dried the streets sodden by the rain which had fallen throughout the night.

The day was March 23rd, 1957, and was to be the last in the life of a twenty-nine-year-old university student sentenced for the murder of a fourteen-year-old schoolgirl.

The calendar had moved forward eighteen months from the time of Burton Abbott's arrest and the confusion of his trial. But even at this late hour there was, I knew, just a slim chance that the condemned man might yet escape—if the telephone rang.

On the winding drive up from San Francisco I had thought about Burton Abbott's last chance and wondered if he himself was still capable of hoping. I was aware that Goodwin Knight, the Governor, was under pressure from many quarters to grant a stay of execution, but he had not moved, and time was running out—fast.

I did not want to think too much about Abbott sitting in his cell victimised by uncertainty, and as I approached the spur of land on which San Quentin stands—jutting into the Bay of San Francisco—I could see, farther out, the misty outline of another penitentiary—Alcatraz. It is an island fortress lapped by tides too strong for any swimmer to overcome.

But I was not interested in Alcatraz and its inviolate record; I was interested only in Burton Abbott, whose death I was going to watch.

I knew I had yielded to a morbid instinct, but executioners, jailers, police officers, coroners, doctors, reporters and many other public servants are all victims of morbidity.

I, too had once been a lawman, Sheriff of Marin County, and when I retired I became a police court reporter. It was how I had become immersed in the case of Burton Abbott versus The People of the State of California, for I had listened to it from its first formal hearing at the Alameda County Court through to the trial by jury.

Throughout his ordeal Burton Abbott had protested his innocence, and I knew, or believed I knew, the exact weight of the evidence against him and the strength and tenacity of his defence.

At the gate of San Quentin I could see a post office, and wondered who cared most—the men whose letters were posted here or those who received them and the telltale postmarks. There was a gift shop close by, filled with leather purses and wooden trays made by the inmates. Before I entered the inspection office I did what I realised later many an incoming prisoner must do—I took a long look across the bay and saw the passing of two ferry-boats.

A security officer accompanied me across the prison yard to the warden's office, where I was checked in as a witness to the execution of Burton Abbott.

Death Row, where the condemned wait out their last days, was on the top floor of the North Block, and when I left the warden's office a guard showed me the way. Before we reached the elevator we were stopped and I was asked to hand over anything made of metal that I was carrying. I surrendered my pocket-knife, nail file, keys and a few coins and was told to collect them on my way out.

As the elevator climbed to the sixth floor I asked the guard if it would be used to take Abbott down to the execution cellar. He nodded, not being very talkative.

The cell of the condemned man was not more than a few paces from the elevator-shaft and I found myself looking once more at a face I had seen many times. I have seen the look of desperation on many faces, but until I stared at Abbott that morning I had not known the meaning of absolute defeat.

He was dressed in new dark blue dungarees and a cotton T-shirt.

Before him was a chessboard whose presence I am sure he had forgotten. He was hunched over the edge of his cot, his body tense and his hands caught tightly between his knees as if awaiting a call. He was, I could see, in the fearful grip of desperate thought, and it had so frozen him that I was reminded of a cataleptic I had once seen, leaning on a broom like a statue, in a hospital corridor he had been ordered to sweep.

When I left Burton Abbott I knew that soon he would follow, unless a message came through from the Governor. The smell of death permeated the whole of the North Block, and it was strongest in the cellar itself, which was well lighted and looked surgically clean and aseptic. It was a smell easy to recognise, but different somehow to that which I had met with many times on the hills, where death had overtaken a traveller, or in some wrecked automobile.

I joined the others in the small observation room and heard someone say that Abbott was at this moment probably being stripped for the last time and searched for any hidden weapons. He was not going to be allowed to pull a fast one. It was unthinkable. No prisoner could be his own executioner.

There was quite a crowd. Prison officials, state and county representatives and newspapermen.

I eased forward to the thick glass window that looked into the gas chamber. It was octagonal and painted an Oriental green. It was, in fact, a metal box designed to contain the cyanide gas that tore the lungs to a bloody pulp. There were two chairs inside that could be used for a double execution, but today Abbott would have to go it alone.

I do not know how long it was I stood at the window, because time no longer meant anything to me, but I felt my nerves tingle when I saw the prisoner and three others enter a tiny cell next to the gas chamber.

I caught sight of a mattress and a toilet bowl without a lid and then realised that one of the guards I had seen earlier, the most jovial-looking, was actually the executioner.

Other people entered the observation room, and we stood pressed together, eyeing the executioner getting everything ready. He took a tin can, full of sulphuric acid, from a closet he unlocked and then carefully filled a metal container with exactly eighty-six fluid ounces of the poison. Now it only needed the turn of a switch and the acid would run through a pipe into a tank beneath the perforated chair that Abbott would occupy.

That was only half the trick, though, for the real turn of the screw came from sixteen pellets of cyanide, each of an ounce, which the executioner popped into a yellow cloth bag and hooked to the end of a long pole suspended over the tank of sulphuric acid. Now everything was ready down to the last deadly detail.

It was as simple as automation could ever be. Push a button and the acid would rush into the tank; pull a switch and the sack of cyanide pellets would fall into the acid. When the pellets met the acid enough gas would be generated to wipe out a regiment, let alone one man.

I had the feeling that I was watching a puppet show when Abbott was led into the gas chamber by the warden, followed by two guards and a priest. I could see the play as Abbott, between two guards, walked to the chair. He looked first at the floor, then at the ceiling, and he needed a little help to get into the chair, but he made it. Without a protest he allowed himself to be pinioned, and soon he was sitting there with his arms and legs encased in broad straps.

The priest stood close to him as a doctor now entered the chamber and fixed a stethoscope to his chest. From it trailed a long tube, the end of which was pushed through a small hole in the wall and picked up outside. From a point of safety the doctor could listen to the heart beat for as long as it lasted. It was important to know the exact moment of death.

I glanced at the telephone on the wall of the observation room and tried to recall a case, any case, in which clemency with crippled steps had overtaken Death, but I was no longer capable of thinking clearly; I could only feel.

I looked through the window again and saw the warden talking to Abbott. As he spoke he took away the cigarette from the lips of the doomed man. He would be telling him, pleading with him, not to fight the gas; to breathe deeply and quickly and help himself to die.

Nothing now remained to be said or done. They had Abbott in the chair, bound and submissive, and now it was up to him. The gas chamber had emptied of all but the prisoner. He was alone in a metal coffin.

The warden and the priest came into the observation room, which had become hot and airless. Everybody waited for the warden to give the signal. He paced back and forth close to the telephone on the wall. He wanted to be able to reach it at once. The instrument did not speak, and the warden looked at his watch. He stepped between the spectators, who made way for him, to the window. His eyes searched the gas chamber. Everything was as proper as it could ever be. Once again he looked at his watch and moved back within reach of the telephone.

It was eleven-seventeen precisely.

If time could have unwound itself to something like eighteen months before, it would have gone back to an hour on June 15th, 1955, when that hot day was coming to its close and bringing the cool of evening. In San Francisco people from their suntrap apartments on Russian Hill and Telegraph Hill probably watched a fogbank as it drifted far out to sea and occasionally hid the setting sun.

Fifteen miles away, and across the bay to the east, lay Alameda, a small isthmus on the Oakland side. Here, too, people were thankful that the sun was going down. In a white stucco house, near to the naval base, Mr. and Mrs. Burton K. Abbott were having a drink with Otto Dezman, a friend and the owner of a beauty shop at which Georgia Abbott worked.

Dezman looked as warm as he felt, and said plaintively that he hoped the heat-wave would not last too long. Georgia smiled, with a toss of her red hair. "If you think it was hot today, you should have tried working at your shop. I was sorry for the women under the driers. They came out as if they had been fried. The weather is bad for business and there were a lot of cancellations. It might be as well to think about putting in some air-conditioning."

Bud Abbott, as his friends called him, came into the room with a fresh tray of ice. He had caught Georgia's last remark and said: "It was bad, too, at the university. Everybody was griping, except the students from the deep South. They're used to it."

"How are the studies going?" asked Dezman.

"Oh, all right, I guess. I prefer the courses on accountancy. They're easier to grasp, but I'll be glad when I graduate and can get a job. I'm under a lot of pressure at the university and it gets me down sometimes."

Georgia moved over to her husband and put her arms around him. "Poor Bud, the heat must be awful for you."

"Chest still bother you?" asked Dezman sympathetically.

"Yep, sometimes, but I guess a fellow can't expect to have a lung and six ribs removed and still be as fit as a fiddle, unless it's a fiddle with a few strings missing."

They laughed at that one as Bud handed round the ice.

Georgia told Dezman that earlier that year her husband had felt very ill and had gone back to the hospital. He was examined and was assured that he was not in need of any further treatment. "It's a good sign, don't you think?" she asked.

Dezman said he thought it was, and the conversation drifted to other topics and finally to a costume party to which all three had been invited.

Bud, with a grin, said he was going to wear an old and tattered suit and go as a university student. "What are you going to wear, Georgia?" he asked.

His wife smiled. "Think I'll go as a Gibson girl. I have a lovely old hat that belonged to Aunt Martha. I just hope it isn't too crushed. While you mix me another drink I'll take a peek in the cellar. I know it's in one of the trunks."

In less than three minutes, though, Georgia was back in the living-room looking white and scared. She was breathing quickly, having run up the stairs. She had a red leather wallet in her hand and she burst out: "I'm sure this belongs to Stephanie Bryan."

Bud looked a bit blank, and Georgia explained that Stephanie was a girl who had been reported missing.

"Are you sure one of your friends didn't leave it behind?" asked Bud, but his wife shook her head.

"Toss it over to me," said Bud, and he began to examine the wallet. Inside it were some pictures and a card that bore the name of Stephanie Bryan.

Dezman took the wallet from his hand as Georgia insisted that the name in it was that of the young girl the police were searching for.

Dezman looked serious. "I think Georgia's right. This snap looks like the newspaper photos. But how in the world did you find it, Georgia?"

"In the cellar. Bud, I think we should call the police right away."

"Go ahead and call them, but please tell me what all this is about.

I haven't seen a paper lately. I've been studying, not reading local scandal."

While Georgia made the call to the Oakland police Dezman explained.

"I don't know how you missed it. The papers have been full of it. The last week in April . . . I think it was the 28th . . . Stephanie Bryan and a friend left the Willard School when it closed at three o'clock."

"How old were the girls?" interrupted Bud.

"I think the papers said they were fourteen. They both stopped at the public library and Stephanie took out some books. Later they dropped into a pet shop and Stephanie bought a pamphlet on the care of parakeets. When they reached the Claremont Hotel the girls parted. Stephanie said she was going to cut through the hotel gardens to her home on the canyon road. Nobody has seen or heard from her since, and the police in Alameda and Contra Costa County have been searching for her ever since."

"Gee, that's sad," said Abbott. "She looks a pretty little thing, if this is anything like her."

Dezman glanced at the snapshot once more. "She is better looking than this from newspaper pictures. Really beautiful."

"No clues at all?"

"Well, something turned up. Seems a man found a French textbook on the roadside up in Contra Costa County. It was wet and he tore off the jacket and gave the book to his son. A week later someone noticed Stephanie's name on the flyleaf and reported it to the police. Since then there have been no new developments."

Georgia returned from telephoning and sat drumming nervously on the side of her glass with manicured fingernails. Bud, though, was calm and began to work on the crossword puzzle in the *San Francisco Chronicle*. "What's a three-letter word for 'to soak'?" he asked.

No one answered, but Georgia looked across at him. He had a face that was handsome and sensitive. Her husband was seven years younger. Dezman, too, was preoccupied.

Georgia, however, soon had a little problem on her hands. It was Chris, her four-year-old son, who called out from the back door that he was feeling wet. So he was, for he had taken a dive into a portable swimming pool. Georgia had just finished feeding him and putting him to bed when the doorbell rang. It was Inspector Charles O'Meara.

He looked at the wallet that Georgia handed to him and then turned to Abbott and asked: "Can you tell me where you were on April 28th?"

"Let's see . . . April 28th. . . . Oh, that's easy. I left here at eleven in the morning to go to the family cabin in the Trinity Alps, in Trinity County. It was the opening day of the fishing season. Remember, Georgia?"

"Of course I remember. I had Mrs. Frakes put up food for you."

"And who is Mrs. Frakes?"

"She's our housekeeper and baby-sitter who takes care of Chris, our son. I work as a beautician and my husband is a student at the university."

Dezman identified himself and the inspector glanced once more at Abbott. The student was back at his crossword puzzle, apparently completely disinterested in the interrogation and unaware, too, of what conclusions might be drawn from the finding of the wallet in his home, which was eight miles distant from where the missing girl was last seen.

"Well, I guess that's all for now," said the inspector. "It's getting late, but we'll be back in the morning."

When he had gone Abbott yawned. "It seems a lot of nonsense, but it's a bit strange. Georgia, how about fixing some sandwiches and getting another bottle of bourbon. I feel like a game of chess. How about it, Otto?"

The next day was much cooler, and even if Georgia had spent a sleepless night she was quite cheerful. Although she could not forget about the red wallet as she lay in bed she had heard her husband and Otto laughing and talking as they played chess, and the noise reassured her. When she got up she was sure that she had been needlessly anxious.

Inspector O'Meara showed up a little later, and I was with him as a police reporter.

The house was modest but tidy and Mrs. Abbott looked charming in a cotton dress whose tints matched the bright glow of her hair. But Abbott looked tired and explained that he had stayed up late with his chess partner. "Beat him, though," he said.

"Mind if we look around?" asked O'Meara.

"Why not? Make yourselves at home. Georgia will show you where she found the wallet."

O'Meara had two other men waiting whose task it was to search the other rooms. I followed the inspector down to the cellar with Mrs. Abbott to take notes. One part of it, underneath the stairs, had not been cemented over, and Mrs. Abbott explained that her husband intended to complete the job when he had the time and energy.

O'Meara looked around and then knelt under the stairs and began to prod into the loose sand. Looking over his shoulder he said to me: "Dave, hand me that shovel over there in the corner." I gave it to him.

The inspector had to work in a cramped space, but he managed to manipulate the spade. Georgia Abbott watched in silence, her hands cupped together as if she were praying.

"Come and look at this, Dave," said O'Meara after a few minutes. I edged in closer and found that he had unearthed a pair of horn-rimmed spectacles. He picked them up with a handkerchief and handed them to me. He continued to dig, and other things came to light—a white nylon brassière, a pamphlet on parakeets and then a red purse.

"Are these yours?" the inspector asked Mrs. Abbott.

She was very pale and said: "No, I have never seen them before. I cannot imagine how they have come to be buried here."

I opened the purse and emptied the contents on the cement . . . comb, pen, pencil, eraser, three pennies, an unfinished letter to "Dear Teddy," and a card of identification for Stephanie Bryan.

Inspector O'Meara was apparently satisfied there was nothing else to be unearthed and we went upstairs. Mrs. Abbott again said she could not understand how the articles could have got there.

"What have you to say, Mr. Abbott?" asked O'Meara as he laid the things on a coffee table.

Abbott looked astonished. "I haven't the vaguest idea."

"Do you keep the basement locked?"

"No, it is open at all times. We lock only the kitchen door that leads down to it." Abbott appeared mystified and bewildered, but he was not at all excited.

"The basement was used as a polling station during the recent municipal elections. You don't suppose somebody put the stuff down there during that time?" asked Abbott.

"What do you think?"

"Well, I just don't know. It's hard to figure, unless someone was playing a dreadful trick . . . or was trying to frame me. These things do belong to the missing girl, don't they?" He made a move to pick up the identification card, but O'Meara caught hold of his hand.

"Don't touch anything. They may have fingerprints on them. Yes, they belong to Stephanie Bryan, as you can see from the card. Guess you'd better come down to headquarters with us for a statement."

Georgia gave a little cry and moved to the side of her husband. "Darling," she said, "you don't know anything about this, do you?"

Abbott smiled and reached for his wife's hand. "Of course not. You don't think if I had known anything I should be dumb enough to hide her brassière and gear in my own basement?"

Abbott had expressed what I had been thinking. If there was any link between him and the missing girl, he had had plenty of time, even up to the previous night, for disposing of her belongings. He could have put them on the fire, or tossed them into the bay. Was it feasible that he had just sat calmly playing chess with his friend and ignoring a peril? Either he was totally unaware that they were casually hidden in the basement or he entertained some rich idea of his own intelligence and believed there was safety in the obvious.

O'Meara instructed one of the detectives to examine Abbott's car. As he made preparations to leave the inspector told Georgia that he would like her to come along as well.

"Of course I will," she said. "I'll just get my hat and bag."

In less than half an hour we were all at the station, and Bud Abbott made a statement that was taken down by a police stenographer. He added nothing new to what he had already said. He claimed that he did not know how the articles had reached the basement and that until the wallet was found by his wife he was not even aware that a girl was missing. He was unruffled and confident and again explained the circumstances of his fishing trip.

"Anyone see you on the trip who can substantiate your story?" asked the inspector.

"I guess so," said Bud. "There were lots of people. As I told you, I left home about eleven. My brother Mark was interested in some land adjoining mine so I drove into Sacramento and tried to find the Bureau of Land Management. Guess I spent about forty minutes getting tied up in those one-way streets, and finally I became disgusted and drove back to the Davis junction. It is a cut-off on 99 W by the Nut Tree restaurant."

Inspector O'Meara nodded.

"When I got to Dunnigan, it was around two-thirty, so I stopped at a little restaurant on the road and had a sandwich. At five-thirty or so I filled up with gas at Corning. I stopped again in Red Bluff for a sandwich, but it was getting late and clouding up so I made it fast on the last forty-five miles to Wildwood. It was around eight-thirty when I got up into the mountains. I stopped for a drink at Delbert Cox's bar and then went to the cabin.

"It had snowed eight to ten inches a few days before, and as it had not rained much I cleared a lot of it around the cabin next morning. I went fishing until it rained, and then went into Wildwood to phone my brother. I spent the rest of the day and evening in Cox's bar. Mark came up with Mary, his wife, on the morning of the 30th, and the following day, May 1st, we all drove home in the rain."

"May 1st . . . h'm," said the inspector, and I knew what he had in mind. It was on May 2nd that Stephanie's textbook was found on the Contra Costa road, one of the roads Abbott might have taken from Trinity County, which he claimed to have visited on his way down.

The rest of the morning was spent in questioning Abbott. He told the same story without any variation, and Georgia became annoyed as she realised which way the wind was blowing. "This is ridiculous," she said. "Abbott had nothing to do with the missing girl. Why would he want to kidnap a fourteen-year-old?"

"Ever hear about sex crimes?" asked the inspector.

Georgia's eyes flashed. "You've got a dirty mind," she stormed. "My husband is a family man. He doesn't have to leave home to search for sex. How dare you infer such a thing."

"I didn't infer anything," retorted O'Meara. "I merely asked you a question."

Georgia believed in her husband, that day and throughout the weeks and months that followed. They were sent home, but warned to remain in Alameda—just in case.

O'Meara and I went out for a cup of coffee. "What do you think about all this mess?" he said to me. "You've been a sheriff and should have some idea."

"Well, it doesn't seem feasible that an intelligent guy like Abbott would leave the girl's personal effects around if he had done her any harm. We are not certain that any crime has been committed. Stephanie may just have run away from home."

"That could be, but I don't think so. Her family background is good. Dr. Bryan, her father, is a radiologist at the university and Stephanie is the eldest of five and a happy youngster. There was no trouble at school, and her friend, Mary Ann Stewart, says that she would have known if anything had been troubling Stephanie. She had no boy friends and no crush on anybody."

We sat there busy with our own thoughts until O'Meara said: "Next step is to take ourselves a trip, Dave. Want to come along? I think we'd better check Abbott's story of his trip and I'll put a call in to the constable in Trinity County."

Back at headquarters, Detective Dean had returned with specimens of lint, threads and dirt he had found in Abbott's grey-green Chevrolet. O'Meara arranged for them to be examined by Dr. Paul Kirk, head of the Criminology Department of the University of California.

The next day four of us drove into the wonderful mountain country of northern California, the Siskyous range that is the boundary between our state and Oregon. The roads there are winding and narrow and occasionally we passed an abandoned shaft—a reminder of past days of gold-mining and of the stories of Mark Twain and Jack London.

The Abbott cabin, we found, was the typical three-room structure, furnished modestly and yielding no fingerprints except those of Abbott. We walked outside and stood looking at the hillside with its company of scrub oak, cedar and white pine. It was tough to know where to start looking.

O'Meara knew his job, however, and half an hour after our arrival a car pulled up at the cabin, filled with local police and a couple of dogs. Three shovels and a pinch bar were taken from the cabin and the owner of the dogs led them over to take a sniff at Stephanie's clothing. It did not take the animals long to make up their minds, and, heads down, they soon made for the underbrush. They crossed and recrossed in quartering the ground and soon they were out of sight, but a few minutes later we heard their howls. We caught up with them on the steep hillside, about a hundred yards behind the Abbott cabin.

"This is the place," said the dog-owner, and we started to dig very carefully. A few inches down we found a brown-and-white saddle shoe and then came on the body of Stephanie Bryan. It was fully clad except that her brassière was missing. Her panties were wound round her neck.

The county coroner was called and the body sent on to Alameda, where it was identified by the parents. As additional confirmation fingerprints and a dental chart were checked and these sealed the grim fact.

Within two hours Burton Abbott was arrested and charged with murder. He was unshaken, though, and said: "Yes, it looks bad for me, and I can see how you fellows are thinking. But I didn't do it. Let's get this thing cleared up so I can get back to normal living."

Without any hesitation he turned over the clothes he said he had worn on his fishing trip. "Bring them down, Georgia. You will find them in the closet . . . you know, the old blue jeans and leather jacket."

Later he asked to speak to Inspector O'Meara. "This is all mixed up," he said. "Let me talk to Dr. and Mrs. Bryan. I want to tell them that I had nothing to do with the death of their daughter."

O'Meara looked sharply at Abbott. "You will have time to see them later when you tell your story before a jury."

The trial started in Berkeley on November 7th, 1955, before Superior Court Judge Charles Wade Shook and a jury of seven men and five women, and throughout the following weeks a posse of newspapermen, including myself, wrote many thousands of words.

It was plain from the start that the prosecution had a problem on its hands, for although Abbott was indicted on the state's Lindbergh kidnapping law, and also for the death of Stephanie Bryan, it was unable to produce a weapon or an eye-witness, or even to prove motive and opportunity.

Abbott looked amazed when J. Frank Coakley, Alameda County district attorney, opened the case by describing him as "a vain, egotistical man who can kill and lie without shame." The prisoner's brow furrowed, too, when it was explained to the jury that a person could be convicted on circumstantial evidence alone.

The parade of witnesses then began. Mary Ann Stewart identified the red wallet as belonging to Stephanie and described their last walk home from school together. A librarian listed the books Stephanie had taken out, and then an oculist produced the prescription for the girl's glasses which tallied with those found in the Abbott basement.

A surprise witness was William Russell, aged thirty-one, who said that he had seen Abbott in Pring's doughnut shop at two-forty-five on the day Stephanie disappeared. Half an hour later Abbott had driven away in a Chevrolet. The shop in question was one of a cluster at the base of the Claremont Hotel, where the two girls had parted.

It was damaging testimony, but counsel for the defence, Stanley Whitney and Harold Hove, succeeded in showing that Russell was an unreliable witness, and they managed to imply that he had been accused by his own mother of knowing more about Stephanie's disappearance than he would say. They could not show, however, any connection between Abbott and the witness that might indicate a motive for a "frame."

Marion Morgan, another witness, swore that Abbott's car almost collided with her own at an intersection near the Claremont Hotel and that he was driving "as if he was going to a fire."

This evidence was intended to spike Abbott's statement that at three o'clock that day he was already well on his way to the Trinity Alps, but it has to be remembered that a Chevrolet of the type and colour that Abbott owned is not uncommon, nor is the human eye infallible.

Eight other witnesses claimed that he or she had seen a couple struggling in a grey-green car parked on the shoulder of a road which leads past the Claremont Hotel, but only one of them was able to say that the girl was "undoubtedly" Stephanie Bryan.

The defence hastened to point out that the spot was popular with young lovers. It certainly had a fine view of San Francisco Bay if one wanted to look at the scenery.

Delbert Cox, owner of the Wildwood Bar in Trinity County, said Abbott appeared at the bar the day after Stephanie's disappearance, but admitted that he had been engrossed in a television show the previous evening and might not have seen Abbott if he had dropped in for a drink before going on to the cabin.

Dr. George S. Loquvan, an Oakland pathologist who carried out the autopsy, said since the body had lain in the wet soil of Trinity County until June 20th he was unable to say how long had elapsed between the girl's death and her burial, or even if she had been out-raged.

When Otto Dezman had described the events at the Abbott home on the evening when Georgia had found the wallet in the cellar he was cross-examined by Stanley Whitney about the possibility of his having hid the articles where they were found because of an attraction for the wife of the accused. This suggestion infuriated Dezman, and, red in the face, he left the witness-stand shouting: "No! No!"

Inspector O'Meara gave evidence on the time element in driving from Alameda to Trinity County. The outward journey had taken nine and a half hours and the return five and a half. Abbott's claim that it took him eight hours was therefore easily possible.

At this point, the defence asked that the jury should be permitted to visit the cabin. It was unthinkable, counsel asserted, that a person with Abbott's physical limitations, the result of a grave operation, could have lugged a body weighing 105 pounds up a steep hill to its burial place. Although the judge turned down the request a good point had been made.

The testimony of Dr. Paul Kirk of the University of California took up considerable time, for he was asked to clarify the evidence he offered respecting the analysis and examination of various speci-mens made on behalf of the prosecution. He made the following points.

Deep in the floor-mat of Abbott's car he found evidence of hair and blood, but it was impossible to say that the blood was Stepha-nie's.

He could find no traces in the car of the girl's fingerprints.

Eighteen fibres and two human hairs were vacuumed from the Chevrolet and the hairs were indistinguishable from Stephanie's hair. The odds were 125,000 to one that they came from the girl's head. One fibre matched her turquoise skirt and several matched her sweater.

By precipitation tests it was proved that soil found on the moun-tain boots belonging to Abbott came from a depth of nine inches of the girl's grave.

Sand from the basement of his home was found in brown oxfords belonging to the accused.

Thirty hairs from the girl's eyebrows and eyelashes were found on her panties and pointed to the garment having been used to blindfold her before it was wrapped round her neck.

Cleansing tissues found in the grave were identical to those in the car.

For three days the court-room looked like a laboratory. The judge, jury and counsel peered at specimens through microscopes, checked samples and, in fact, took a course on crime detection as exemplified by the newest scientific methods.

It was a bit overwhelming for everybody, and one evening a few of us went to San Francisco to get away from it all. Sure enough, though, we had no sooner settled in the little restaurant which was a favourite of mine when one of the newspaper boys said: "I can't figure out the deal. Why should Abbott leave all that evidence lying around if he had killed the girl. I think he's been framed."

I played the heavy father. "You reporters were just kids when the Loeb and Leopold case made the headlines. Remember, they were two rich and clever students who killed a young boy just for the thrill of it? Crime is often inexplicable, at least superficially."

Another of the boys had a point and he made it. "It could be that somebody killed the girl and planted her belongings in the cellar. The cellar was always open and plenty of people were aware it could be entered. Why not the nut who may have done it?"

It was a possibility, and if that were the truth of it Bud Abbott had become the victim of a chain of vicious circumstances.

Next I had a talk with Mrs. Elsie Abbott, who was Bud's mother. It would have been inhuman not to have felt sorry for her. She said bitterly: "We have raised fifteen thousand dollars to defend Bud, but I can see we need more help . . . scientific help. I know my son is innocent, but we need to rebut the kind of evidence given by Dr. Kirk. The way things are going in the case it seems to me that justice is based on how much money you can call on."

It having become apparent that the defence intended to exploit the suggestion that Abbott was incapable of carrying Stephanie's body the prosecution called Dr. Elmer J. Shabart, of the Livermore Veterans' Hospital, where the accused was operated on in 1951. The witness said Abbott had called at the hospital five days after the girl had vanished and asked for further surgery. "He seemed almost over-anxious, but we told him that another operation was not necessary. On May 13th he again called."

The district attorney smiled at the jury. "Case for the prosecution rests," he said.

It was a case which provoked a lot of controversy, in the home and throughout the country. If there were many who condemned Abbott as a crass and unfeeling killer there were also many who believed him innocent and the victim of cruel error.

The trial now rested in the hands of the defence, and counsel set about the task of knocking the props from under those witnesses called for the prosecution. For every piece of damaging testimony thus provided the defence produced its antidote.

Two waitresses from Pring's doughnut shop testified that they had not seen Abbott in the shop on the day of Stephanie's disappearance, nor William Russell, who said he was there.

Walter Raleigh Bethel, aged seventy, claimed he had seen a struggle between a girl and a man in a parked car. "I cannot say who the girl was, but I can say the man was not Abbott. I think Abbott is being framed."

"Objection," roared the district attorney. "The witness must not give the court his opinions."

"Objection sustained," said the judge. "Strike out the last statement from the record."

A truck driver and vegetable salesman both swore they had seen the young girl in a restaurant in the company of two Mexicans on the night she disappeared.

Police Sergeant Cyril Smith, uncle of the accused, said his nephew had invited him to the cabin for the opening of the fishing season. It was evidence which showed that the trip to the mountains had been planned before the crime took place.

The housekeeper to the Abbotts, Mrs. Hilda Frakes, said that the day before the trip she helped Mr. Abbott to pack. She saw Abbott on May 3rd, after his return, and he was not marked in any way, either by scratches or bruises.

The witness was asked if Mrs. Abbott possessed any blue jumpers, and she said that her mistress had both blue and white jumpers, as indeed did their young son.

"Is the basement always unlocked?"

"Yes, it is always left open."

"Have you ever known strangers to enter?"

"Well, I cannot be sure, but one day in the spring Chris went down the stairs. I heard him let out a scream and he ran back to me and hid in my skirts. He couldn't tell me what had happened, but I felt that probably he had been frightened by a prowler. . . . No, I don't know when this happened."

The day Burton Abbott gave evidence the court was packed. He was, as I have indicated already, very handsome, and there were as many men among those who believed in him as there were women. He had fine eyes and his manner was sober and quiet. He adhered to his previous explanations . . . with two exceptions.

"I did not go to Sacramento to look for the Bureau of Land Management as I have said. That was a lie. I promised Mark I would investiagate the property, and I didn't want him to know I had let him down. Other than that, the events of April 28th were exactly as I have told you."

"You have heard the testimony of Dr. Kirk that samples matching that of the girl's grave have been found on your mountain boots. How do you explain that?"

"Very simply. When I was up in the cabin in June, more than a month after the girl's disappearance, I prowled all over those hills. . . ."

"What about the sand from the basement that was found in your oxfords? You have previously said you were not down in the basement."

"That is right. I said I never go there, but I had forgotten that one morning Chris threw one of his toy cars down the steps and I had to get it for him from under the steps. It was such a little thing that it completely slipped my mind."

At the end of four days Abbott appeared to be at the end of his strength. The interrogation had dragged on, and while his memory had been excellent to begin with it was no longer so. He began to fall back on "I do not remember" and "I cannot recall" and when he stepped down at last he was pale, weary and shaken.

Although James A. Craig, garage owner, could not positively identify Abbott, he told the court he had serviced a car with an unusual red fan-belt such as the one on Abbott's Chevrolet. The time was somewhere around 5.30 p.m. and some two hundred miles away from the Claremont Hotel.

The waitress and the owner of the Chuck Wagon Diner at Red Bluff said Abbott had eaten there at seven-thirty on the evening of April 28th. The pretty little waitress fixed the date as the day before she left her job.

Yet another witness, Robert Wetzel, said he had seen the garage doors ajar at the mountain cabin late on the vital evening. Since the doors were always locked, it showed that someone was there. A man and his wife swore that earlier they had waved a grey-green Chevrolet over the narrow bridge at Wildwood.

Mary Abbott, Bud's sister-in-law, denied a prosecution suggestion that he possessed additional mountain clothes other than those he had handed over to the police, and Tom Daly, a mill worker, said he had had a nine-hour session over a bottle with Bud on April 29th. But drunk or sober, Abbott was, claimed the witness, quite normal and his usual self.

The trial, now in its second month, was adjourned for four days over Christmas, the jury being instructed by the judge not to discuss the case with anyone or to listen to the radio or look at the television or the newspapers. The verdict they would have to give, said the judge, must be made on the unbiased and uncontaminated judgment they, each one of them and jointly, would reach.

When the court resumed the defence produced two further witnesses, Ed Jepperson (Bud's brother-in-law) and his stepson, seventeen-year-old Pete Ford.

"It is impossible for Bud to have had mud on his boots from April," said the younger witness. "I saw him wash them off in a sluice-box in June. Whatever dirt was found must have come from our hunting trip afterwards. Dr. Kirk must have made a mistake."

It could not have been much of a Christmas for relatives of the accused man. They, no doubt, had not only searched their consciences, but their pockets. There was not much of the defence funds left, but Mrs. Elsie Abbott was a fighter and produced in court Lowell W. Bradford, criminologist to Santa Clara County.

He was a big man, of impeccable reputation, and had once been a student of Dr. Kirk, the prosecution's expert. Bradford did not go as far as to contradict his teacher, but he added a few more questions to the many the jury would have to consider.

He produced, for instance, two fibres identical to those secured from the sweater of the dead girl. One had been found in the car belonging to Mark Abbott and the other in the fishing-box which the accused owned. Neither of the fibres could have got to where they were found during the time of the kidnapping and murder.

Then Frank W. Barley, a soil chemist, stepped on to the stand and scoffed at the suggestion that the soil on Abbott's hunting boots came from the victim's grave. With the aid of a microscope he showed that the soil samples were not even of the same colour.

On December 31st the defence rested, but the procession of witnesses was not yet over, for the prosecution still had a card or two left.

Mrs. Bessie Wells said she knew Burton Abbott.

"Did you see him on April 28th?"

"Yes, I did."

"Will you please describe the circumstances."

"On the afternoon of April 28th, I was having a permanent at the Dezman beauty shop. Mr. Abbott came in to speak to his wife. I waved to him. It was between two-fifteen and two-thirty."

There was a buzz in court and spectators sensed that this was the "kill." Yet another witness was on hand—Mrs. Leona Dezman, Otto Dezman's wife, and manager of the shop. She swore that Abbott came into the shop twice on the crucial day; at 10 a.m. and in the afternoon at two-thirty.

Defence Attorney Hove, cross-examining, asked Mrs. Dezman if she was not lying out of revenge against Georgia Abbott for refusing to cover up an affair she (Georgia) was having. Was it not the case that Mrs. Dezman was shielding her husband and his possible guilt in framing Bud Abbott?

The defence made much of the possibility of a "frame" without being able to point a finger at the culprit, and on January 19th the jury retired. For seven days these men and women were closeted together with court records, transcripts of the testimony and recollections of what had been said by the prosecution, the defence and the judge. In the evenings they were taken to their quarters in the Claremont Hotel, where from rooms lit by chandeliers they could look down on the lovely gardens below, at the very place where Stephanie was last seen alive.

Police escorts took the jurors to and from the hotel. They were chaperoned during meals and protected from all interference. They were not allowed to receive telephone calls, nor to read any newspaper.

On the seventh day the foreman of the jury told the judge a decision had been reached and the courtroom was prepared to hear the verdict. Abbott looked white and apprehensive and his counsel on either side were slumped in their chairs. The two Mrs. Abbotts, mother and wife, both dressed in black, sat with clenched hands.

The foreman said:

"Your Honour, after careful study and due consideration, we, the jury, find the defendant Burton Abbott guilty of murder in the first degree. It is our recommendation that he be granted no mercy from this court."

There was a roar in court and the judge rapped for order. Mrs. Elsie Abbott looked towards her son, her face twisted in anguish.

As I pushed my way through to get to a telephone I stumbled against the foreman of the jury.

"How do you feel about this?" I asked.

The foreman looked me over. "He is a mad dog, and should be eliminated."

"May I quote you?"

"You may."

It was February before Abbott was sentenced to die in the San Quentin gas chamber and taken to a cell in Death Row. Opinion on the verdict was by no means unanimous, and an appeal was lodged. Two notable lawyers came to the support of a young man who had been convicted by a carefully woven web of circumstantial evidence. They were Leo Sullivan, who volunteered to prepare the appeal, and George T. Davis, a masterly tactician of judicial procedure. The Abbott family was more than grateful, for the cost of the trial had weighed heavily on them. With renewed hope everybody lent a hand. Bud Abbott's aunt, Mona Marsh, typed the transcripts and a cousin in the printing business reproduced copies of the appeal.

But two incidents occurred that were disquieting, even sinister. In May original documents in the case vanished from the office of the county clerk and have never been found. A month later a bundle of documents "twice the size of a telephone book" was stolen from Attorney Leo Sullivan's unlocked hotel room. The lawyer was staggered and asserted bluntly that both thefts had been planned by someone who wanted to get Abbott gassed.

The thefts certainly provoked a lot of argument. People plagued both Sullivan and Davis with letters and telephone calls. Some were friendly, some were anonymous and threatening.

In the appeal heard by the Supreme Court, Attorney Sullivan presented a 162-page brief in which he accused the police of withholding vital evidence and alleged that some witnesses were browbeaten, lied to and even threatened. In reply District Attorney Coakley referred to the accusations as intangible and utter nonsense. All the efforts of Burton Abbott's new defenders could not upset the jury verdict, and in upholding the death sentence the appeal court declared that the evidence at the trial was clearly sufficient to support the judgment.

Abbott's mother refused to be daunted by this setback. I had become familiar to her among the reporters who had stayed on the case and she sent for me. "I do not for one minute believe my boy is guilty," she said. "Somewhere there is someone who can prove his innocence. I want you to arrange for an advertisement in your paper offering a reward of two thousand five hundred dollars for information establishing the innocence of Bud." Mrs. Abbott was a wonderful mother and it was impossible not to be deeply moved by everything she said and did. Other papers in the Bay area took up the advertisement, but no one came forward and by now Abbott had been in Death Row for over a year and the end was in sight.

With the failure of the appeal George T. Davis played the last card in his hand—he appealed to Governor Goodwin Knight to grant a stay of execution, a plea made formally and in an appearance on television.

The hands of the clock are moving round. It is eleven-seventeen and thirty seconds.

We are under the spell of unbearable tension. We, the crowd in the observation room, do not move, and each can hear the whistle of another's breathing. I had known all along that there was no absolute certainty that Abbott was guilty. Now that he was on the threshold of death I felt the full horror of unsureness. The telephone would not ring—it was, like us, paralysed.

At eleven-eighteen the executioner pushed the button and I swear

I heard the acid rushing into the tank under Abbott's chair. Almost with the same movement the executioner pulled the other switch and fused the chemical formulae.

We stared through the window at the Dantesque scene. A cloud of cyanide gas swirled upwards and enveloped Abbott in a gauze of haziness. He began to strain at his bonds and jerked his head back to get out of death's way. I couldn't see his face, the gas was pouring out, but I saw the desperate twist of his body, upwards and then to each side. It was no good, and suddenly he lay back motionless.

Eleven-twenty . . . The telephone began to ring and, dazedly, the warden took the receiver off the hook on the wall. Somebody from Sacramento was saying that Governor Goodwin Knight had granted a stay of execution. The message had been radioed from an aircraft far out at sea on which the Governor was taking a trip.

It was two minutes to the second too late.

Body in the Baggage

by Ex-Police Chief Etienne Levecque, Marseilles, France

"MON DIEU, but it is terribly hot again today. This weather has become unbearable," complained Sergeant Beauregarde, wiping the perspiration from his face with a limp handkerchief. From my desk next to his I glowered at him through a haze which played tricks with the room itself. The walls appeared as if they were trembling and ready to disintegrate at any moment.

"What do you expect in Marseilles in August—a snow-storm?" I asked in exasperation. "I have been in this department for over ten years and every summer it is the same. It is hot, sticky and utterly miserable, and has to be endured."

We both mopped our brows and tacitly agreed that the conditions were too stifling for further conversation. I glanced again at the list that lay before me. It offered no solace and was merely a routine record of routine happenings. In order of priority were a couple of waterfront incidents in which an irate mistress had brained her lover with a bottle and an English tourist had "lost" his wallet prowling the *bistros* in search of a girl and the inevitably crummy bedroom. The chump had got what he deserved, I concluded, and this was one "adventure" about which he would not care to tell his cronies. There was little else on the list except the usual batch of minor offences, pilfering and the like. It occurred to me that for a busy, bustling port Marseilles was unusually quiet and law-abiding. It must be the sun; it tamed everybody—even criminals.

It was at this precise moment that the telephone rang on a sus-

tained note, imperious and impatient, and it was the introduction
to one of the strangest cases I have ever been called upon to in-
vestigate during my career as an *agent de ville*. The call was from
an agitated stationmaster at the terminal. He was worried, very
worried, over some luggage deposited for shipment on the *Ile d' Yeu,*
due to leave for England the next day.

"Come on, Pierre," I said to Sergeant Beauregarde. "Forget the
heat and put on your coat. We're going to the railway station."
He looked pleased. "Fine! We can take the first train to Paris. Think
of all the pleasant things we can do there."

"Stop clowning," I rebuked him. "This is strictly business."

We drove to the terminal and walked into the luggage office.
The stationmaster was waiting for us, and so, too, was a porter
named Jacques Hart. He looked as if he had seen an apparition.

"Aha, gentlemen, thank you for coming so promptly," said the
stationmaster. "Jacques here will tell you what the trouble is."
The pale face of the porter became a little paler, but he was not a
man to shirk his duty.

"Well, monsieur," he said to me, "today a lady and gentleman
asked me to see that their luggage, a trunk, travelling bag and
hatbox, were placed on the *Ile d' Yeu.* I looked at it some time
after they had gone. There seemed to be something oozing out of the
seams and the smell was really awful. It made me feel quite ill."
Jacques shivered, and it looked to me as if he might not last out
the interview.

"Are those the pieces?" I asked somewhat prophetically, point-
ing to some luggage isolated at the end of the room.

"Oui, Monsieur Levecque."

It was unnecessary to move in closer to catch the sickening
odour which had so upset the porter. Whatever the luggage contained it was certainly not perfume.

"This is no place in which to begin work," I said. "We need
ventilation and a cool atmosphere. We'll get this luggage out of
here before it becomes too ripe to handle."

I could see that Jacques now felt that he had done all that could
reasonably be expected of him, but to his credit he made no protest
when I suggested that he should accompany us.

At the morgue Dr. Aristide Bergoud, white-coated, stood eyeing the luggage as he told his assistant to lay the three pieces on a large table.

"The trunk, we'll have that opened first," said the police surgeon with what I thought was quiet resignation.

There are some things one never forgets, and, as the lid of the trunk was lifted, my skin still crawls to this day when I remember what I saw and how the smell of a charnel-house became horribly more pungent. It was like opening the furnace door within a crematorium and still being shocked, though one had no right to be.

What now faced us was the torso of a woman—a stump with a bosom and arms. The hands were narrow and finely moulded and the long fingers seemed to point regretfully to the foreshortened thighs and the bloody nullity of amputation.

I remember wondering what kind of knife had been used to achieve such mutilation and if the murderer had had a saw handy as does every butcher when cutting up a carcass.

After a brief examination Dr. Bergoud pointed silently to the travelling bag that he knew must contain the legs, and, finally, of course, there was the hatbox, which with simple and diabolical logic had been reserved for the head of the victim. No woman sleeps with her hair in disarray, and this poor creature, although she slept eternally, had her blonde tresses drawn backwards and tied at the nape with a strip of crimson ribbon. The forehead, high and intelligent, dominated a face which had serenity and seemed indifferent to Fate.

Dr. Bergoud sighed, and I could well understand what lay behind his mood, for I, too, felt that sometimes it is hard not to loathe the human race.

I left him at his work and walked into another room where Jacques, the porter, was waiting. Usually I have a drink when the day's work is done, and not before, but I had seen too much to care about a lifelong habit and sent Beauregarde out for a bottle of Chablis. I gave Jacques a glass and said to him: "Tell me, what do you remember of the couple who left the luggage with you?"

"I am certain the woman was French, but not her companion. He was tall, very thin and a foreigner of some sort."

"What makes you so sure?"

Jacques smiled a little sadly. He pulled out a ten-franc note and said: "He gave me this, which is much more than is usually offered

by any of our countrymen. Madame was very French—Parisian,
I think, from the way she talked, nineteen to the dozen."

"Do you recollect how they were dressed?"

Jacques thought for a moment before answering. "Monsieur's
clothes were expensive, but he dressed carelessly. His tie was made
in a slovenly way and there was a large stain on his coat. Madame
was *très élégante*. I believe her dress was silk. Her coat was very
fashionable and she wore a large hat and carried a huge handbag."

"About what age were they?"

"He was probably between fifty and sixty, but I think she was
younger. She looked it, but you can never be certain of women,"
he said a bit ruefully, as if he had had some experience. "She wanted
the luggage sent on to Boulogne and then shipped across to Dover
for delivery in London. Here is the address."

As I handed it over to Sergeant Beauregarde and told him to ask
Scotland Yard to check it for us, Dr. Bergoud came into the room
and sat down wearily.

"The head isn't as pretty as it appeared," he said grimly. "At
the back of it there are several wounds and a severe occipital
fracture."

Unlike myself, Dr. Bergoud had finished for the day. He accepted
the glass of wine I handed him and went on to give me his other
findings.

"The age of the victim was somewhere between thirty-five and
thirty-seven. She was a natural blonde, possibly German or Scandi-
navian. Apart from the head wounds she had been stabbed in the
back several times and by an instrument that doesn't appear to
have been as sharp as a knife. Death occurred less than forty-eight
hours ago, and there are traces of blood and skin under her nails
which indicate that she put up a fierce struggle against her killer.
The dismemberment was accomplished less by surgery than by
butchery."

The doctor took an appreciative sip of his wine. "There is no
evidence," he continued, "of sexual outrage. And that, Inspector,
is all I can tell you for the time being. Is there a question you would
care to ask?"

"Yes," I said without hesitation. "Who did it?"

Dr. Bergoud chuckled and got to his feet. "That, my dear sir,
is *your* little problem. As for me, I'm going home to take a bath."

It was with some envy that I watched him leave, for his day had ended and mine had a long way to go. After dismissing Jacques with a warning that we might need him again, I set two squads of detectives to work; one under Sergeant Beauregarde to track down the driver of any vehicle who might have taken the suspects to the terminus, the other under Sergeant Blanc to check every hotel and *pension* to see if they were still in Marseilles.

Back at headquarters, I had a meal sent up and waited around until ten o'clock that night, but nothing further developed. The next morning Sergeant Beauregarde had something to report. Scotland Yard had discovered that the address given on the labels of the murder luggage was fictitious. I was not surprised. The other news was that two persons had been located who could tell us something about the couple for whom we were searching.

The first witness was a tiny, shrivelled individual who had driven the couple from the railway station to the Hôtel du Louvre et de la Paix.

"Oui, I remember them, Monsieur le Préfet," he said. "I could hardly forget so soon. He gave me a large tip and Madame was a fine figure indeed. She looked like a duchess."

The cabby was sure the man was a foreigner. When I asked him to explain he replied with a smile: "Well, he didn't protest when I asked for double the fare I usually charge."

The other informant was the assistant manager of the Hôtel du Louvre et de la Paix.

"You want to know about Mr. and Mrs. Jarvis, as they called themselves," he began at once. "We received their reservation by telegram from Cannes the day before yesterday. I met them upon their arrival and took them to their suite. Madame did a great deal of talking and knew what she wanted."

"Such as?" I interrupted.

"She told me at once that she would not occupy a suite without a bathroom. Of course, that is only natural in this weather. She inquired about the service and the food, and it was obvious that nothing but the best would satisfy her. I was puzzled, though, by the fact that Monsieur had no luggage and neither did his wife, except a jewel-case which she would not allow out of her sight."

He paused as if he still had an ace up his sleeve, but before he could continue I asked him if he thought the couple had registered under a false name. "Yes," he answered, "that was my impression. The jewel-case was decorated with a crest and monogrammed. I noticed the initials were 'M. St. L. G.' and it didn't suggest her name was Jarvis. She appeared to be an aristocrat, and I was sure she was having a gay time and just wished to be discreet about it."

"A gay time indeed!" I said. "Don't you know why we are trying to trace this couple?"

"No, the sergeant didn't tell me." He was no longer quite so self-assured as he waited for me to explain.

"They are wanted in connection with a gruesome murder, and, naturally, we want all the help we can get."

He was astounded. "It's hard to associate a woman of her quality with murder," he said. "I can't believe she would do such a thing. Perhaps the man, but surely not her."

"Aren't you just being chivalrous or did Mr. Jarvis appear sinister?"

His voice dropped into a confidential whisper. "Monsieur had been drinking. I am sure it was whisky and the smell of it almost knocked me over."

"It doesn't necessarily indicate that he was a murderer; but tell me what happened."

"Well, the Jarvises retired to their suite and then ordered lunch to be served in their rooms. Monsieur wanted a cab to be at their disposal immediately after lunch. It was obvious that he was not French and had great difficulty in explaining what he wanted. Madame intervened and told me they intended visiting a friend, an officer on a cruiser in Toulon. They left and I have not seen them since."

I scribbled an instruction to Beauregarde to obtain a list of the permits issued to visitors at the naval base during the last two days and could hear him on the telephone putting through the inquiry.

There was nothing more to be got out of the assistant manager, but I had a feeling that we had moved in a little closer to the suspects and posted a detective in the foyer of the hotel they had deserted to nab them if they returned—which I doubted.

Sergeant Beauregarde discovered that no permits had been granted to anyone by the name of Jarvis, nor indeed to anyone answering their description. He had, though, found the driver of a cabriolet who had taken Mr. and Mrs. Jarvis to Toulon. He had been hand-

somely tipped, but all he had to impart was that he had dropped his
fares at the Hotel Toulon.

We rang the hotel. The Jarvises were not staying there and nobody seemed to have noticed them. It was at this thwarting moment
that Dr. Bergoud arrived. He had made a second examination and
told me that the body had not been dismembered until about eighteen
hours after the murder. He was very observant was Dr. Bergoud, and
had noticed that the blanket in which the torso had been wrapped
bore the name of a Montreal hotel. Some of the packing had been
done with newspapers, both French and English.

All this was very interesting, but hardly illuminating, and, as
the case stood at the moment, it seemed to me to be full of unrealisa-
ble possibilities. We had an unidentified corpse of whom we knew
absolutely nothing, neither her nationality nor even the place where
she had been done to death, and we had a couple of suspects travelling incognito and doing it so cleverly that they appeared to have
given us the slip. I was not greatly worried, because the hour was a
little early and the tracks were still fresh—if we could recognise
them. But what puzzled me was that the stylish Mrs. Jarvis was
travelling around apparently with little more than a change of ear-
rings. She must have a wardrobe somewhere, and its discovery
could indeed provide a short cut to our laying hands on her.

Sergeant Beauregarde seemed to have forgotten the weather in
the heat of the case. He was indefatigable, and from his inquiries
we learned that the murder luggage had been unloaded from the
van of a train from the Riviera which had made several stops on
its journey to Marseilles. Secondly, the telegram making the hotel
reservation for the Jarvises had been sent from Cannes by the
steward of the night train.

This gave us something to get our teeth into, and we telegraphed
the police at Cannes and other coast resorts to find out if the couple
had anywhere arranged for the dispatch of the luggage.

In no time at all replies came tumbling on to my desk. They were
all discouragingly negative—not a lead anywhere, that is, until I
got a telephone call from Cannes from a police officer who was an
old colleague of mine.

"Etienne," he said, "I think I have some news for you. I questioned the railway porters here myself, and it seems that a large and

expensive bag, well spattered with French and English hotel labels, was expressed out of here five days ago."

He kept me on the hook for a few moments just for the devil of it, until I said impatiently: "Yes, yes, but what else?"

He chuckled and said: "Perhaps you will be interested to know that the bag was addressed to Mrs. V. Jarvis at La Ciotat, care of the luggage depot."

The fog was beginning to lift, of that I was certain, and perhaps this is what had happened. The Jarvises had boarded the train at Cannes together with the murder luggage. The hotel reservation at Marseilles was just an expediency so that they could arrange for the shipment of the body. Having done so, they had then gone on to Toulon just to cover their trail. From Toulon they would by now have gone to La Ciotat to catch up with the piece of luggage which had been forwarded there. The place lay about midway between the naval base and Marseilles.

"Beauregarde," I said, "clear up your desk. We are going to La Ciotat, and who knows but that we may run down our quarry there."

The sergeant looked pleased and responded by shoving the assorted files and papers into the top drawer of his desk. He then took out his handkerchief and carefully dusted off the scored wood. He looked at me for approval.

Our route was La Grande Corniche, the southern coast of France, and it was a delight to leave behind the broiling city and feel the cool breeze that blew in from the sea.

As we approached La Ciotat much later that day I began to wonder if I had not grasped at a straw too optimistically, but consoled myself with the thought that in a murder investigation one picks up a crumb here and there like a sparrow on a winter's day. We found the bag at the station—a handsome affair made of alligator skin, plastered with stickers, and with an address tag which showed that it belonged to a Mrs. V. Jarvis. I must confess that I gave it a cautious sniff—it was a little habit I had picked up recently from handling luggage.

It was, however, as fresh as a May day, its contents faintly perfumed in a well-bred way; lingerie, silk dresses, stockings and all the armoury of feminine seduction, but not a label on any of the garments. Nor did the bag contain a letter or an address of any kind.

I was telephoning the local police to arrange for a man to be posted in the luggage office to keep watch for anyone calling for the bag when Beauregarde opened the door of the booth and pushed into my hand a little bottle he had found among the powders and pomades. Aptly enough it was full of little pills to be taken for headache and had been bought from a pharmacist in Monte Carlo. It was another crumb, but I waited until we returned to Marseilles before telephoning M. Blanchard, prefect of police at the famous resort.

I explained to him the case of the body in the baggage and finally told him of the clue we had picked up at La Ciotat.

"I have a few things to clear up here, but soon we shall be on our way to Monte Carlo and by the time we arrive perhaps you will have something to tell us."

"You may depend on it that I will do what I can."

I knew Monte Carlo, of course, but not as a visitor. Then, as now, it was exclusive and expensive—the bejewelled crown, so to speak, of Monaco the miniature and washed by an incredibly azure Mediterranean. It was the magnet for gamblers and adventurers; men on the look-out for rich women, rich women on the look-out for young men. In the interests of survival Monaco possessed a small but clever police force to protect an international set loaded with money and jewels.

Monsieur le Préfet was awaiting us when we arrived the following day, and I could tell that he had been very busy.

"Gentlemen, I think I have some useful information for you. From your description of the victim, Monsieur Levecque, it may well be that she is none other than Madame Elsa Livén, a young and wealthy widow, who has been staying here for some time. She has been missing from her hotel since last Thursday. She is Swedish, blonde and looks much younger than her age, which is thirty-seven. Although she visited the Casino almost every night she was known as a careful player.

"Last Tuesday she drew a large sum of money from the bank and also took some of her jewels from the vault and returned others she had taken on a previous visit. It was her usual custom to take various pieces to match the clothes she intended to wear."

"Monsieur Blanchard," I said, "we are indeed indebted to you.

I think the next move is to try and establish identification. Can you suggest anyone we can send to Marseilles to look at the body?"

The prefect smiled. "After talking to you yesterday I was convinced that the victim was Madame Livén, and so I took the liberty of sending the head porter of the hotel on the morning train to Marseilles. We shall soon hear from him."

I nodded, and M. Blanchard added:

"As for the Jarvis couple, their description would fit any number of visitors here. It seems to me that the majority of foreigners are all tall and thin. There are, too, many gay, talkative and fashionable women in Monte Carlo.

"I sent a detective to the pharmacy, but he drew a blank. Such pills as you mentioned can be bought anywhere, and a headache in Monte Carlo is not an uncommon experience!"

Sergeant Beauregarde had listened attentively to the conversation, and, nudging me with a bony elbow, he whispered the word "whisky." I knew what he meant, and told M. Blanchard that our male quarry generally left a strong smell of whisky behind him. He had to buy it from somewhere.

The prefect replied: "It isn't much of a clue, but it's worth looking into." We divided Monte Carlo between us and set about the task of interviewing everyone who sold wines and liqueurs.

The shopkeepers I questioned were both surprised and wary when I asked if they had a foreign customer to whom they sold whisky. It was plain to see that they suspected the imminence of a new tax. Finally, though, a woman talked freely.

"I sell a lot of whisky to Lady Goold and her husband, the English baronet and financier," she said. "I believe they used to live in Canada, and that is probably where they got the taste for it. Not everyone cares for it. They take a bottle nearly every day and it's good for business, but at the moment they owe me a large bill and I have not seen them for a few days."

I thanked her, secured the address of the villa the Goolds were occupying, and bought a bottle of champagne in return for the information. It was nearly noon and time for lunch with the prefect and Beauregarde. I felt the champagne could well be used for the occasion, since the information I had secured fitted those facts we already knew. The "G" on the jewel-case which the assistant manager of the hotel in Marseilles had seen in the possession of Mrs. Jarvis could stand for Goold, and the blanket around the victim's torso once belonged to a Montreal hotel.

The luncheon was excellent, the first meal I had really enjoyed since the discovery of the dismembered body. The restaurant, of pink stucco, overlooked the sapphire Mediterranean. The sun was warm but a strong breeze shook the sun-umbrellas which shaded the tables on the veranda outside. The champagne bucket glittered in the pure light; the onion soup and the *omelette avec champignons* were the best I have ever tasted. Perhaps all this sounds callous and unfeeling, but what would happen to crime investigation if detectives allowed their private feelings too much rein?

We got back to the case over coffee, and then the three of us drove in a barouche to the address I had been given. The Goold villa was small and seemed to hug the hill on which it stood as if it feared to slip into the sea.

There was not a bell, but a great knocker capable of waking the dead. The door was answered by a pretty girl whom I judged to be in her twenties. I told her we wanted to see Lady Goold and her husband, and without hesitation she replied: "I'm sorry, but my aunt and uncle are away visiting friends. I am Henriette Duval, their niece. Perhaps I can help you."

"It is your uncle I particularly want to see. This is just a routine call we are making on every foreign visitor to find out how long they intend to stay."

The young girl smiled. "I don't know how much longer we shall be here, but you should ask Aunt Marie when she returns. I am sure she will be able to tell you rather than Uncle Vere." She was of course telling us that it was her aunt who was the family spokesman. We thanked her and and said we would call on another occasion.

We returned to the office of the prefect to learn that the hotel porter had identified the body as that of Mme Livén and from other inquiries we now knew, too, that the handsome young widow was a friend of Sir Vere and Lady Goold. I had decided to return to headquarters, and leave it to M. Blanchard to tip us off when the Goolds returned to their villa, when the telephone rang. It was a personal call from Marseilles with news from La Ciotat.

That day a servant had called at the station to pick up the alligator bag. He had presented a claim check and also a note from Mrs. Jarvis authorising him to collect it. He was trailed from the station to a mansion overlooking the beach and it was being watched until our arrival.

It was not possible to arrive in La Ciotat until the following day, but everything was in readiness and a detective led us to the house on the cliffs. A servant in livery opened the door and I could see just within the hall the long, lean and swaying figure of the man I knew was our quarry. I stepped past the servant and said in English: "Mr. Jarvis, I have come from Marseilles to see you about some luggage you were intending to ship to England. I am sure you will understand that it is necessary for both you and your wife to return to Marseilles with us."

He looked bemused, and had obviously started the day early—drinking.

"See here," he said, "you can leave my wife out of this. And, incidentally, my name isn't Jarvis, as you suggest."

With a slight stagger he straightened up and added haughtily: "I don't think you appreciate you are talking to Sir Vere Goold. I am a financier and extremely well known."

"I understand that you have been staying in Monte Carlo?"

"Yes, until recently," he replied, eyeing me warily.

Before I could put another question to him Lady Goold came down the staircase, looking precisely as everybody had described her, regal and exquisitely groomed.

"What is all this about?" she said in the manner of the well-bred addressing an intrusive scullion.

Stung by her arrogance I answered sharply: "Madame, I am here to take you both to Marseilles. You are wanted on suspicion of murder."

"Come, Vere," she said, trying to encourage her ashen-faced husband. "Compose yourself. There is nothing to be concerned over. This boor is merely carrying out the instructions of his superior."

That really rankled, and I could not resist turning to Sergeant Beauregarde and saying: "I am sure Madame has a jewel-case that is worth looking at. Please get it from her maid and we'll take it along with us."

She gave me a cool stare, but nevertheless I knew that I had shaken her confidence. Beauregarde quickly reappeared with both the jewel-case and the alligator bag, which had been packed in readiness, but hardly for a visit to Marseilles.

It was no trouble at all to hump the cases into the cab, but Sir Vere took a little hoisting and slumped down silently in his seat next to Beauregarde. The baronet immediately took a pull from a silver flask he was carrying.

The journey from La Ciotat to Marseilles was not remarkable for scintillating conversation. Lady Goold was not her old self, and it must have been a rare experience for her to find that she had nothing to say. Sir Vere every now and then took a bracer from the flask, and when Sergeant Beauregarde glanced questioningly at me, I shook my head, knowing that it was perhaps wiser not to interfere with the baronet's habit of fortifying himself. Indeed we stopped along the way when the whisky ran out and he wanted to buy another bottle.

Many hours later we reached Marseilles. Lady Goold entered her cell with the dignity of a Christian martyr submitting to her persecutors, and she did not speak to her husband at the moment of parting. I do not think Sir Vere was in a condition to speak even had he wanted to, and he was pleased to stretch himself on the bed of his cell in the men's section.

"When our baronet gets thirsty tomorrow," I said to Beauregarde, "he'll talk. In any case we'll give both of them the chance to think awhile before we question them. I want to see Henriette Duval, and we'll have to send for her. She must not be told the reason why the Goolds have been arrested."

She was waiting for me after lunch the next day, and the poor girl looked terribly worried. As kindly as possible I asked her to tell me all she could about her aunt and uncle. It was easy to see that she was greatly attached to them, and she had lived with them for some time, in fact since the death of her mother, who was Lady Goold's sister.

"I don't know what the problem is," said Henriette Duval, "but I am afraid I am involved in it. I know I have been a great disappointment to my aunt and uncle. You see," and she blushed, "they were really counting on my marrying a rich husband. It's the reason why we have spent so much time in Monte Carlo, but eligible men are scarce.

"Aunt Marie has done everything to help. She insisted on renting an expensive villa and has spent far more than she could afford on my clothes. Nothing was too good for me, and she would not allow me to help with any domestic work because she feared my hands would become coarsened. I have suspected for some time that their money was running out. Is it because of this that they have been arrested?"

I avoided the question by asking: "Tell me, has anything happened at the villa recently that has appeared strange to you?"

Henriette thought for a moment and then said: "Yes, something occurred which I thought was a little odd. Aunt Marie kept me out of the villa for two afternoons not long ago. She did so by arranging that I should do some shopping for her, but they were silly little errands and I realised I had been sent on them for a purpose."

"Did you notice anything when you returned on those afternoons?"

Henriette considered the question. "Yes, I did. On both occasions my aunt was wearing an apron as if she had been doing some housework, which was, of course, very unusual. It puzzled me until I remembered that she had discussed selling the last of her jewels. I thought she must be upset and that she had turned to doing something in the house, as women often do when they are under some strain."

It was quite clear that Henriette had no inkling of the real reason why it had been necessary for the villa to be free of her presence on the two afternoons of which she had spoken.

It took some little time, but eventually, and with the help of the Paris Sûreté, Scotland Yard and other sources a dossier was prepared on the Goolds.

Lady Goold was actually the daughter of working-class parents and had been apprenticed to a fashionable Paris dressmaker. She had an instinctive feeling for elegance and might easily have become famous in Paris as a dress designer had she not hastily married a rich but irresponsible young man. She was then eighteen, very good-looking and vivacious. The young couple moved to Geneva, where Marie Girodin, as she had become, exploited her talent as a *couturière* and a flair for mixing with her social betters. She made a lot of money, but out of some capriciousness she left her husband quite suddenly and was next heard of in Bombay. Here she showed socialites the art of French chic and successfully transplanted herself. She understood much more about clothes than she did about men, and having been divorced she chose for a second husband a dashing British officer, a certain Captain Wilkinson, who ran through her money and left her penniless within three years. Again she became a divorcee, but she was still young and attractive and not without courage. She left Bombay for London, succeeded in business once more, and was comparatively well off when Sir Vere St. Leger Goold laid siege to her and she fell without a shot being fired. She undoubtedly was dazzled by his social eminence, impeccable manners and personal charm, otherwise she would not have omitted to inquire if he could afford to keep her in the manner to which she had occasionally been accustomed. Sir Vere was not only penniless but a toper, and the marriage had lasted four years when the Goolds sailed for Canada to avoid a lost legion of creditors.

They returned after several years, not to England though, but to France. Marie Goold's sister had died and there was nobody left to care for Henriette Duval. Marie thought that she saw a way out of their dilemma. They would find a husband not only rich enough to secure the future of her pretty niece but with enough money to support Sir Vere and herself.

The idea was hardly original, nor was it at all successful, for they found that although Monte Carlo sheltered many rich men the competition was overwhelming. Of calling cards there were but few, but of bills there were many, and they became increasingly importunate.

That was the background to the Goold history, a story to be understood in its wider implications by the brutal facts of the murder itself. We knew that the Monte Carlo police had found in more than one room of the Goold villa unmistakable traces of blood.

The case had its complications. Sir Vere was a British subject, and the crime had been committed in Monaco, while the place of custody was Marseilles. It was ultimately decided that the couple should be arraigned under French law. At the preliminary hearing by the examining magistrate poor Henriette Duval sat in the corner of the room looking pathetically pale and nervous.

She heard Dr. Bergoud testify that he had examined Lady Goold on her arrest and had found scratches on her neck and throat. Placed before the magistrate was Lady Goold's jewel-case, and it contained pieces that a bank clerk of the Crédit Lyonnais was able to

identify as the property of Mme Livén. His testimony was simple but
damning. He said:

"On Thursday, August 1st, Madame Livén, whom I knew well,
drew out a large sum of money. She had deposited with the bank
a quantity of jewels, and some of these she took away with her.
She told me that she had selected the finest pieces as she had been
invited to see a collection owned by Lady Vere Goold."

The evidence was being taken on deposition, and, as the scratch-
ing of the court pen ceased, the bank clerk, answering further questions put by the magistrate, said:

"Madame Livén asked my advice about the proper wording of a
promissory note. She said she had agreed to lend Lady Goold the
sum of twenty thousand francs to help the family over a temporary
difficulty. Sir Vere Goold was waiting for a *coup* to materialize. Madame Livén said she was not certain what security she would be
offered, but it was possible that instead of a note being arranged she
would accept some of Lady Goold's jewels as security."

The magistrate looked at the prisoners for an explanation. They
both denied that any arrangement had been made to borrow money
from the victim.

During the course of the hearing the prisoners were taken sepa-
rately to view the body of Mme Livén. Dr. Bergoud had so arranged
the limbs that although the cadaver was complete in a sense, it
was obvious that butchery had been done. The head had been placed
a little to one side as if the rest of the body had become an insup-
portable burden.

Lady Goold turned quickly away from the sight, but for her husband the corpse appeared to possess a terrible fascination. He stared
at it without speaking, and slowly his shoulders began to hunch
and his body, so it seemed, began to shrink. His face had become
twisted as if pain had so triumphed over him that he was powerless
to protest. Somewhere from the depths of his being there began a
scream like the mortal howl of a wild animal. He began to stagger
about, drunk with fear, and had to be led away. When the terror
had drained out of him he began to mutter a confession. He alone
was the murderer, he said. He had outraged Mme Livén and had
then killed her and cut up her body so that it could be more easily
disposed of. The crime had been committed in an alcoholic frenzy.

The confession did not fit the facts. The body showed no signs of

sexual assault, although it could hardly be doubted that Sir Vere
was his usual tipsy self at the time of the murder. Lady Goold
scoffed at her husband's explanation. His mind, she said, had become unhinged by his being deprived of alcohol.

The trial was held in Monaco, and in the meantime Lady Goold
had given some consideration to her predicament. She was, she said,
prepared to explain exactly what had happened.

"I have been guilty of a frightful mistake and of obstructing
justice," she said. "On that terrible afternoon Elsa Livén and I were
having tea together, and both Vere and Henriette were out. Without
warning, a swarthy, powerful man burst into the room. I had never
seen him before and I could not understand what he was saying.
He had a hammer in his hand and turned suddenly on poor Elsa and
struck her down. When he saw he had killed her he ran out.

"I became panic-stricken, as I knew the murder in my house
would ruin us socially, no matter how innocent we were. I thought
that if we could get rid of the body it would save us from utter disaster. I persuaded Vere to help me when he returned, and together
we cut up poor Elsa's body. We hid the pieces in the trunk room
at first and later tried to dispose of them in Marseilles."

It was left to Sir Vere to tell the court the truth. He admitted that
the invitation to Mme Livén to inspect the jewels which were purportedly to be offered as collateral for a loan was part of the plot. At
five o'clock, as prearranged, he crept into the room where Madame
Livén was being entertained and struck her on the back of the head
with a coal-hammer. It was not, however, a fatal blow, and she
fought back, clawing at Marie. In the struggle he again struck her
with the hammer and finished her off by stabbing her with a paper-
knife.

By the time Henriette returned they had hidden the body and
done their best to clean up the room. The dismemberment took place
the following day and then preparations were made for the trip to
Marseilles.

Sir Vere Goold was sentenced to imprisonment for life, but a more
condign punishment was reserved for his wife. It was decreed that
Marie should die by the guillotine. It is difficult to understand the
court's judgment, but evidently it was of the opinion that it was
Marie who really inspired the murder.

She was the first woman ever to die in Monaco in this way, and a

guillotine had to be borrowed from France to carry out the execution. On January 14th, 1908, the head of Marie Girodin Wilkinson
St. Leger Goold—as the French revolutionaries would have said—
sneezed into the basket in retribution for the head which had been
packed so neatly in a hatbox.

The Cat Man of Honolulu

by Ex-Police Chief Richard Kam

I REMEMBER how dead Mr. Yamashiro looked when I pulled him out of the fishpond of his favourite tea-garden into which he had fallen from having drunk too much *saké* and not enough tea . . . it was a ridiculous mistake for a staid businessman to make, and, I am sure, Mr. Yamashiro would have agreed had he been in a position to discuss the matter. As it was he just stank, poor fellow, overwhelmingly of *saké* and had nothing to say; I remember, too, how morally indignant Pedro da Silva was when he gave me an account, and a very full one, of how he had beaten his wife almost to death in a cane plantation one day. Pedro spoke eloquently, always with a musical downbeat of his expressive hands, as he explained how it had come about that he had been provoked into murderous rage. His wife had committed the unbelievable and unpardonable folly of serving him a dish of rice cold . . . such is the inner complexity of human nature that Pedro, cuckolded on countless occasions, as well as being robbed and cheated by his greedy spouse, had never thought to take a stick to her until she outraged not his honour but his appetite.

From the foregoing you will understand my dilemma when I was asked to recall some outstanding story that had happened during my years as a police chief. The fate of Mr. Yamashiro and the confession of Pedro da Silva are probably duplicated, with certain variations, every day, everywhere. Likewise the occurrences at those houses of questionable reputation in Waikiki, which many visit out of boredom and leave in dismay. I am assured that among the peculiar happenings there were incidents full of comic disaster, but I do not think they are suitable for telling in a book of this sort.

In any event I want to tell a story that in itself could happen perhaps only in Honolulu—a gentle story, even a little amusing, but one with a happy ending.

The first chapter, so to speak, began one night when I was called to an apartment house near to the Queen's Hospital. My assistant, Lieutenant Kahali, accompanied me, and we found a young and beautiful girl, Miss Eva Ching, very frightened and in tears. She told us that she had not long undressed and got into bed when she saw a man in the act of crawling through the window, which she had left open. In her terror she screamed, and, without saying a word, the intruder retreated, jumped over the hibiscus and croton bushes outside and vanished.

"Miss Ching," I asked, "have you any idea why your house should be invaded in this way?"

The Chinese do not cry easily, and already her almond eyes had become dark and inscrutable, but she was still shocked, as I could see from the paleness of her face. She did not answer immediately, but stood silently considering my question. She was as slim and graceful as a willow and was wearing not the barbarous tunic inflicted on our islanders by Boston missionaries many years ago but a straight-cut Oriental robe of shantung that matched the delicate hue of her skin.

"Officer," she said, "I do not know . . . except that today I bought a new piece of jade. Let me show it to you."

We followed her into the living-room. With deft fingers she lit two candles on a low rattan coffee table and turned on a lamp in a corner of the small room. She asked me politely to see that the strong Kona wind did not extinguish the flickering lights.

She left us for a moment to get the jade and I looked around. It was just a well-kept Honolulu apartment. There were pink anthuriums in a blue bowl on the table and lauhala mats on the floor. The *punee,* or couch, was covered with bright pillows. It was pleasant but not opulent, and an enterprising thief could most certainly have found richer homes in Honolulu to rob.

So I thought until I saw Miss Ching's jade. When she opened the carved teak box, I realised that she possessed a small but rare fortune. Each piece was exquisite, and, appropriately, they belonged to a beautiful girl.

"I brought this little collection with me from China," she explained. "In those days my family was well off."

She handed over the box so that I could examine the pieces more closely. "May I touch them?" I asked, and she nodded happily. The ear-rings, brooches and rings had been made many years before and the settings were superb. It was wonderful to touch them.

Miss Ching watched me and then said: "This is the ring I bought today. I have saved up a long time for it."

She opened her long hand to show me a sliver of the loveliest imperial jade I have ever seen. It is quite impossible to describe the tint of imperial jade, but there is, I think, no green anywhere to compare with it.

"This is what he wanted," said Miss Ching sorrowfully.

Hereabouts I should explain that robbery is alien to the character of the people of Hawaii. Not until recent years did anyone dream of securing a door, day or night. The island philosophy was simple and warm-hearted; nobody would take anything that did not belong to them, unless they were in real need of it. If it so happened that they were in need, well, they were welcome to help themselves.

It could be, as Miss Ching thought, that somebody wanted her jade ring, but what was important now was that she should not be left alone, frightened and apprehensive, and so she went to stay with friends for the remainder of the night.

The next night was silvered by a full moon and filled with the sound of the Kona wind, the sick wind as it is called, because it fills one with unease and lays a weight on the spirit. Everywhere doors and windows rattled, palm fronds nodded nervously and the great trees creaked and groaned.

Lieutenant Kahali paced my office restlessly until the telephone rang. The caller was terribly excited, but I managed to get an address from her and Kahali and I hurried to yet another apartment house.

A pretty young woman, Miss Theresa Yashida, was being consoled by those in the house who had heard her scream. She was a schoolteacher and she told us that she had gone to bed shortly after ten o'clock. She had been to a lecture earlier in the evening at the university, which sprawls over the green Manoa Heights, and found herself thinking of what she had heard. Anyhow, she could not sleep and lay gazing at the waving trees she could see beyond the open window which faced her. Then she saw something which paralysed all movement in her. It was the figure of a man, hardly more than a shadow, as he darted across the lawn towards her window. She waited helplessly until his head rose above the sill and at last she was able to call out in terror.

People rushed to her help, and not all of them were convinced that she had not had a nightmare.

"He was like a cat, the way he sprang on to the sill and crouched there on all fours until I screamed, and he fled," Miss Yashida said.

It had been Miss Ching last night and now it was Miss Yashida, and it was obvious that both girls had been visited by the same intruder, the Cat Man of Honolulu, the name he came to be known by.

Then one incident followed another; a nurse awoke from her midnight sleep in readiness for a spell of duty to find a man lying in a twin bed next to her. He was gone before she could raise an alarm; another young woman was awakened by the feeling that she was no longer alone in the darkness. Somebody was watching her. She screamed and a man vaulted out of the window into the night.

People began to bolt their doors and windows, but the Cat Man did not pay indiscriminate visits. He climbed into the bedrooms of young women who were, to say the least, exceedingly personable, but never molested them. Nobody saw him long enough to provide us with a description and nobody complained of any attempt at sexual interference. Nor was robbery the motive. He could have picked up jewels and fineries, but he touched nothing. It was extraordinary.

In the district where he was most active, I arranged for five of our detectives to patrol the area from early evening to early morning. One or two of them saw a shadow, but that was all, and over a month went by in this way without the watchers getting a glimpse of the Cat Man.

Well, not every cat cares for cream, but for the Cat Man ultimately we discovered a "mouse," and a pretty little creature she was indeed. I found her waiting for me one morning and her name was Anne Suzuki. She looked, despite her tininess, extremely professional in the starched uniform of a nurse. She was so small that for a moment I thought she would have to stand on tiptoe in order to see me behind my desk.

She said with rare aplomb: "I can help you catch the Cat Man."

I looked at her and marvelled at her supreme confidence. Only a girl of her inches could possess so much. It seemed that she knew something of what I was thinking, for she added pertly:

"Yes, I can get him for you, but you must promise me that he will come to no harm and that when you arrest him his real name will not be published in the newspapers. You see, he is troubled in his mind and needs to be helped rather than punished."

A little maliciously I asked: "Tell me, how do you intend to arrange for his capture?"

"It is quite simple," she said reprovingly. "He is coming to see me tonight."

No doubt I looked like a tropical fish out of water, and Miss Suzuki smiled and explained: "Last night I found him lying on the bed next to mine. I had awakened quite unexpectedly, and as he ran out of my room I slipped out of bed and called out to him to come back and see me tonight. He stopped and looked back at me. I saw his face, and it was not that of an evil man. He will return, I am sure of it."

This was one girl the Cat Man had not scared, but as we talked over our plans to put an end to his nocturnal prowling she again insisted on a promise from us that he was not to be roughly handled or his real name revealed. I tried to persuade Miss Suzuki that he might show his claws when he was trapped, but she shook her head.

That evening I took two officers along with me to Miss Suzuki's apartment. One of them concealed himself in the bushes outside and I placed the other in a closet in the bedroom. My post was near the light switch where I could watch the little nurse without being seen by anyone sneaking up on the apartment.

Miss Suzuki, without a trace of nerves or excitement, cooked herself a meal of rice and *teriyaki* and sat down to enjoy it. She ate slowly, put the dishes away and later walked into the bathroom. When she came out she had changed. Over her night attire she wore a Japanese robe of brilliant red. Her long hair was caught up by a ribbon, and it occurred to me that whatever else he might lack the Cat Man certainly had an eye for beauty. Miss Suzuki piled up the pillows on her bed and settled down with a book.

Time passed slowly, but not unpleasantly. The moon was brilliant and the sloping lawn shimmered in its light. The Kona wind was still with us, but it was beginning to lose its power. Shortly before midnight Miss Suzuki turned off her reading lamp, went to the double doors, stretched luxuriously, and with a flip of her hair piled into bed.

Ten minutes later I saw a shadow glide through the line of royal palms that marked the yard from the cement pavement. Then a lithe form darted with unbelievable speed across the grass, reached the window and dropped into the room with a soft plop. As the intruder straightened up I switched on the light.

For an individual who had terrorised a lot of girls the Cat Man was hardly impressive. He was less than average height and I judged him to be about twenty. He had a sensitive face, though, delicate hands, and his feet were bare. He wore a green *aloha* shirt, white trousers which had been carefully pressed, and clutched a small bouquet of red roses, as rare and expensive on the island as orchids are elsewhere. They were, of course, intended for Miss Suzuki.

He blinked in the bright light and made no effort to escape, but slowly turned to Miss Suzuki. As he offered the flowers to her he said: "Why did you do this to me? I would not have harmed you."

Miss Suzuki put the flowers on the bed, took hold of the young man's hands, and said very gently: "And we will not do you any harm either. Good will come of this."

She went with us to headquarters and stood protectively by while we booked . . . Manuel de Romero.

We were soon to discover that the Cat Man's luck had by no means run out, for nobody wanted to prefer a charge against him. The girls who were asked to testify could not be sure that he was, in fact, the prowler. Manuel was quiet and rather melancholy and the girls eyed him curiously and not without sympathy. He would not talk much about himself and was handed over to a psychiatric clinic.

It was from this source that we got to know about him. He was born in the isolated fishing village of Kalapana, on the Big Island, Hawaii. His life was quite literally filled with death, for his mother, a handsome woman, was drowned in the treacherous cove of the black sands. Two years later his sister, whom he adored, died of tuberculosis. Manuel's father, a misfit in a fishing village, returned to Portugal, leaving his adolescent son in the care of a Mr. Sung, an aged ascetic, who threw out nets by day and studied by the light of a kerosene lamp at night.

Manuel endured the poverty and loneliness until he was old enough to look after himself. He moved to Honolulu, where he got employment making *leis,* the necklaces of flowers, carnations, pekaki, vanda orchids and the ivory-like crown flowers. It was work he liked, but at the end of each day he would return to his room as lonely as ever and sadly in need of the friendship he was too shy to seek.

"When the sick winds come," he told a doctor, "I get *pilikia* here," and touched his heart.

He swore that in seeking out young women by night he was not impelled by impure motives, and I believe that was an explanation accepted by his psychiatrist. Manuel was really a lonely romantic who still remembered the death of his mother and sister and needed somebody to whom he could transfer his love. There was nothing seriously wrong with him, but he needed help. He found a friend who showed him how to understand himself. She was of course Miss Anne Suzuki. It was an odd courtship in many ways, for Miss Suzuki worked in a ward for neurotics and often of an evening she waited around until Manuel had finished another session with his doctor. Anyhow, the young couple were not too preoccupied to overlook falling in love and they were married when Manuel's problem had evaporated.

Today they are a happy pair and the parents of two children of whom they have every reason to be proud. All goes well with them and I see them often. Once Mrs. de Romero said to me: "If I had screamed as did the others look what I might have missed!"

There is, I think, more than one moral to this story, but the one my people will understand more readily is that although it is delightful to lie by the side of a beautiful girl it is only polite first to ask her permission!

A Machete for Don Victor

by Assistant Police Chief José Mario Quintans, Ecuador

THE BODY of Don Victor Hugo Eguez was found tied to a tree in the Salitre country one day in early November 1950. Don Victor had not died easily. He had been mutilated by the machete, the broad South American blade we use either as a knife or a tool. Don Victor had been a handsome young man before the machete had cut him in ribbons, but he must have proved difficult to kill, because it was a bullet in the back of the head which finished him off. It could have been an act of mercy, the *coup de grâce* of torturers sickened by the sight of suffering and the gouts of blood that spurted from the wounds of the stricken man.

The physical facts of the slaying, fearful as they were, provided the initial shock—yet to come was the real impact of the astounding story . . . the hidden love-abode in the jungle where a beautiful woman awaited the caresses of her lover; the gun battle in the mountains between the hired assassins and the police, and, lastly, the political intrigue to mask the face of murder and scandal.

The final act ended sourly for justice, it is true, but that is a contingency every detective must learn to expect, particularly of a case in which too many people were involved.

It was from my superior, Chief of Police Lucio Terreros, that I first heard of the crime. On the day of its discovery he burst through the door of my office and said in a tone I well understood: "Get your feet off the desk and pretend you're alive. We've a murder on our hands. This is where you justify your salary."

I looked hard at Terreros—he was not being playful, although I knew his snarl was worse than his bite. Nevertheless it was with some irritation that I asked: "Perhaps you'll be good enough to tell me who has been killed."

"Don Victor Hugo Eguez," he answered tersely.

No wonder Terreros was worried and bear-like. Don Victor was the eldest son of one of the richest and most influential families in Guayaquil.

"The body was found tied to a tree near the Road of the Crosses," explained Terreros. "He had been stabbed and shot and I can tell you that it isn't going to be a simple job to find the killers."

Already the corpse had been removed to Salitre, and I asked the chief how the murder had been discovered.

"One of the workers on the Eguez plantation crawled into town this morning with a bullet in his back. His name is Francisco Castro, and it seems that two days ago he was with Don Victor and Firmin Escalante, a Negro servant, riding through the jungle. According to Castro the little party was ambushed and Don Victor kidnapped. Castro was shot while running away and lay in the jungle for some time before he was able to move. He is a powerful fellow, otherwise he would not have survived either the wound or the journey."

"Where was the body of Don Victor found?"

"About ten miles from where he was kidnapped. He had been dead only a few hours."

"Any news of the Negro Escalante?"

"He was Don Victor's personal servant, and so far there is not a trace of him."

It did not take a master mind to understand that Don Victor's kidnappers must have been known to him otherwise it was unlikely they would have killed him. It was improbable that the crime was committed to collect a ransom because the body would most certainly have been buried. Yet something like thirty hours had elapsed between the ambush and the murder. If murder was the only motive why had the killers waited all that time? And stranger still was the disappearance of Firmin Escalante.

Chief Terreros and I began our investigation by having a talk with Major Eguez, Don Victor's father. He had not received a demand for ransom, nor, I judged, would he have paid it under any circumstances. The old man was tough and forthright and not the one to bargain with thieves. The death of his son was a great blow.

"There is something that I do not understand," he said. "My son was to have been married in ten days' time to Teresa Rubira, and yet we have found many love letters in his room from an unknown woman. They were unsigned, and in one of them she says she will kill him if he dares to marry someone else. I know that Teresa did not write them and was unaware there was another woman in his life."

This was putting it mildly, as Detective Francisco Mera found out a little later from Raoul Bolona, a close friend of Don Victor.

"Women in his life? Yes, there were many of them," said Bolona. "Not very long ago he told me of his infatuation for a lovely creature whose name he would not mention. It was a secret he guarded closely. He told me, though, that she was hidden away in the jungle, near to La Palmira, the Eguez plantation, and that he spent as much time with her as he could. As old friends we have often discussed our conquests, discreetly of course, but this time Don Victor was not to be drawn out and I judged it to be a very passionate affair."

Once the preliminary inquiries were completed Terreros and I rode out of town. The Chief was not easy to keep up with. He was mercurial and absolutely tireless, but on the way to the jungle and the Road of the Crosses he pulled back his mount to a trot, waited for me to come up, and said: "All the signs point to a murder of revenge, and it may be that we shall find the killers among the mountain bandits. The machete is their favourite weapon, and Don Victor had more than his share of wounds. He must have been expected at the place where the ambush occurred, and the likely person to have tipped them off is Escalante. It would account for his subsequent disappearance."

"Do you think the woman who wrote the torrid love letters inspired the murder?"

"No, I do not. Bandits don't take on a job like this merely to oblige some jealous woman. They'd want paying, and paying well. There is an explanation we do not yet know."

We found the spot where Don Victor had breathed his last, tethered our horses, and began to search the ground near by as carefully as we could. The work was very unrewarding, but at last I came across an empty bottle that still retained the smell of cheap, immature brandy, but it told me that it could not have been tossed aside many hours ago. Pencilled across the label was the name "La Tuza." It was a hamlet of not more than a dozen houses and a few miles away.

I showed the bottle to Terreros and his eyes gleamed. "It looks as if the killers needed a drink to help them with their dirty work."

I nodded and told him: "Whenever it is safe, bandits use La Tuza to get drink and supplies from a man there named Falquez."

Later that day when we reached the hamlet we found where Don Falquez lived and bought a bottle of brandy from him. It too had the name of La Tuza pencilled across it, and Terreros promptly produced the bottle we had found and said to the liquor-dealer: "Here is the bottle you sold not long ago to the men who killed Don Victor Eguez. I want to know who they were."

Don Falquez excused himself. He was sorry, but he was unable to help, simply because he did not know the men to whom he had sold the brandy. He was obviously scared, but Terreros was accustomed to this kind of situation. Very quietly he asked: "I don't suppose you would like to be arrested as an accomplice of the murderers?"

No, Don Falquez decidedly would not. He shrugged his shoulders, which indicated that he had no choice in the matter. "There were three of them," he explained, "but one of them I do not know. The Franco brothers, Gregorio and Pedro, came first. They often buy drink from me, and that night they bought a bottle of brandy and sat down at the table. They said they were waiting for somebody to whom they wished to talk. I was not to try and listen to the conversation nor even to take as much as a glance at their visitor. They warned me that if I tried to find out who their visitor was it would be the last thing I would ever do.

"This was advice I could not afford to ignore, and when the other man arrived I took little notice and kept out of the way. From the little I saw I am sure he has never been here before."

"But surely there was something about him that you must have observed," insisted Chief Terreros. "You must have been curious and taken a look at him."

"Yes, I did, but I was afraid of the Franco brothers. They are not men to trifle with. The stranger wore a long cloak and he was afraid of being recognised. He kept his head down and spoke quietly. He did not belong to the mountains, but to the town. One could see that from his clothes."

There was no more to be got out of Don Falquez, and we had to be content, but on the journey back we put up a number of handwritten notices offering a reward of 100 sucres for information of the whereabouts of Gregorio and Pedro Franco. I did not think the bait would pay off, but it produced a surprising result.

Within a few hours Pantaleon Franco, the father of the wanted men, read one of the notices pinned to a tree and sought out Chief Terreros.

"You will find my sons in the Black Mountain. That is where they always hide whenever they have done something very bad."

Terreros was curious and asked: "Why are you telling me this?"

The old man looked at him gravely and said: "There was a time when my sons were good boys and gave me no trouble. But they have changed, and now it seems as if they do not care even if they commit murder. This is something that cannot be permitted, and if you find them I want you to put them into jail for eight years. Then perhaps they will return to me afterwards and become good boys again."

Old Pantaleon Franco knew that in our country killers rarely serve a sentence longer than eight years. He had been a good father to his sons, but now he would rather see them in jail than have them commit another murder.

However, Gregorio and Pedro were not so easily taken. We traced them to their mountain hide-out, and were met with a fusillade which told us that the Franco brothers had some help, probably a few of their bandit friends. Terreros had foreseen this and the squad under him took cover and settled down to a gun battle. It went on through most of the day, but in the late afternoon our quarry ran out of ammunition and surrendered.

When we entered their cave Gregorio and Pedro were still on their feet, but there were three dead, among them Firmin Escalante, the Negro. Terreros' hunch that Don Victor's servant had betrayed his master had proved correct.

The brothers had nothing to say when we asked them about Escalante, and they would not reveal the names of the other two men who had been killed that afternoon. They insisted that they had nothing to do with the murder of Don Victor.

The sun was setting when we started back for Salitre, and we had not gone far when Pedro made his last mistake. He made a break, but had run only a few yards when he was riddled with police bullets and died immediately.

Gregorio stared at the body of his brother in the shock of amazement. A moment before Pedro had been alive, a swaggering philosopher who had accepted his capture nonchalantly. Now he lay face downwards with one arm outflung, the span of his life cloven. Gregorio turned a twisted face towards us as if to confirm the incontrovertible fact of Pedro's death.

Terreros saw his opportunity. "But for the man in the long cloak who planned the murder of Don Victor your brother would still be alive," he said. "Tell us, Gregorio, who the man was."

Gregorio looked at Terreros dully, as if he did not quite understand the question. We waited to hear a name—the name of the quiet one who had slyly wrapped himself in a cloak and spun a web of murder.

"It was Don José Antonio Freire," Gregorio said.

Terreros exploded. "Don José Freire!" he shouted. "Are you mad, or do you believe us to be? What would he be doing mixing with bandits? Gregorio, you had better tell the truth."

I could appreciate Terreros' exasperation. Only *El Presidente* was more powerful that Don Freire in all Ecuador. And I remembered, too, that he was actually the father-in-law of Don Victor's sister. It seemed incredible that he could be involved in murder.

Gregorio said wearily: "I did not think you would believe me, but I have spoken the truth and I will swear to it on the Cross. Don Freire was responsible for the murder. It was because of a woman."

"And who is this woman?" Terreros asked cautiously.

"I do not know. I have never heard her name, but Don Freire told us he had hidden her deep in the jungle. He was wildly in love with her and visited her whenever he could get away from his wife. He was happy until the day Don Victor found her. He was young and ardent and Don Freire was at a great disadvantage. The jungle flower wanted only Don Victor.

"It was because he had stolen the woman from him that Don Freire had us kidnap Don Victor. The old man wanted to force him to give up the woman and had him tied to a tree. Don Freire pleaded with him and said he would give him anything he wanted if he would promise to keep away, but the young man would not give in, and Don Freire began to torture him. It went on all through one night and the next day and it was not good to watch.

"But Don Victor was brave, and even when he was being stabbed with a machete he refused to submit. Finally, when he was near to death we shot him through the head."

It was no longer possible to doubt Gregorio's grim confession, but it had to be proved, and the one person alive who could corroborate it was the mystery woman herself. She had to be found. Terreros and I found her after a long search.

Near the Eguez plantation, and shaded by bushes and a belt of trees, we came at last upon a little cottage—the love abode where Don Victor had supplanted his elderly rival. Quite unexpectedly the door opened, and it seemed to me a symbolic act that illumined the present and revealed, too, all that had happened here and in the jungle.

Here, in the bright light of day, stood a woman who was no longer young, but still beautiful enough to inspire murder. She had dark, intelligent eyes and a sensual mouth and when she smiled the sun of her spirit lit up her face. Her lovely shoulders were bare and she wore a dress that obviously was not meant to hide her superb figure. Around her slender throat was a necklace of garnets set in gold.

"*Buenos dias, señores,*" she said softly. "I have been expecting you. Permit me to introduce myself . . . I am Señorita Amada Lopez."

Terreros glanced quickly at me. Of course I had heard of Señorita Amada; indeed, who had not? Her beauty had become almost a legend in Ecuador. Her power had not diminished. She was still able to enslave men, and this was something of which we did not need proof. She talked to us frankly of the passionate attachment between herself and Don Victor and what it had meant to Don José Freire. It clinched the case against the old man, but such was his influence throughout the country that it was not until four years later, in 1954, that he and Gregorio Franco were tried for the murder of Don Victor Eguez.

Both were found guilty, but whereas Don Freire was jailed for one year only, upon Gregorio was visited the full rigour of the law. He was ordered to be imprisoned for eight years.

Matriarch with a Machine Gun

by J. Edgar Hoover, Director F.B.I., Washington, D.C., U.S.A., with Ken Jones

THEY NEVER came any tougher than "Ma" Barker and her brood, and that goes, too, for the other half of the gang—the hoods led by Alvin Karpis. I should know, for I helped to hunt them and, finally, to eliminate them. Of all public enemies they were unquestionably the vilest—a throng of wanton killers, vicious, depraved and incredibly ruthless.

We know all about murder and its motives at the Federal Bureau of Investigation, and possess the records of many men and women who have killed often and inhumanly but yet had a side to their nature that was not wholly despicable.

It is something that cannot be said of "Ma" Barker, her four sons and Karpis, and the mobsters they commanded. Without a single exception they were monsters, and pity was a word of which they had never heard. They moved in a welter of blood; mail robberies, bank hold-ups, kidnapping and pitched machine-gun battles; they loved nothing better than to kill a police officer, and if some innocent bystander fell to the same hail of bullets that did not matter either. They executed their own traitors, bought over unfaithful police officials, "fixed" paroles and prison breaks. Their anarchy fouled the very roots of law and order.

I remember their heyday and the various impressions I received from the tortuous investigation, the interrogation of witnesses, and the study of reports which came in from special agents all over the country. "Ma" Barker, for instance, renting an apartment from an unsuspecting landlord, knowing that if he looked into her hard eyes he would guess the truth; a drunken doctor shaving the fingertips of a crazed hoodlum no longer under an anaesthetic; Karpis, the slit-eyed killer, explaining how he was going to wipe out top F.B.I. agents in Los Angeles, Chicago, New York and myself in Washington by using automobiles and planes, and hating it like hell because somebody had called him a rat; an afternoon search in St. Paul when we were sure we had the gang dead to rights and a flood of sound unexpectedly broke out—church bells, kids yelling and a dog howling.

Yes, Alvin Karpis, otherwise Francis Albin Karpavicz, had dreams of gunning the F.B.I., and never more vivid than at the moment we grabbed him.

So intensely did the Barker-Karpis alliance live by the gun that it is impossible to give an orderly picture of their stained history. They intertwined murder with corruption, but it is probably right to ascribe to "Ma" Barker the gang's inspiration for organised crime. She was born Arizona Donnie Clark of very mixed blood—Scots, Irish and Indian. She grew up in the Ozarks, the wild, mountainous region of Missouri, and among people who were as stark as the scenery. She is supposed to have coached her four sons, Herman, Lloyd, Fred and Arthur, on the principle of how to do business with bankers—with a tommy-gun. But in the beginning she herself had no criminal experience on which to draw. She indulged them, though, wilfully and wickedly, and it is beyond dispute that the four Barker boys owed their criminal careers to their mother. She was both resourceful and ruthless and they looked to her for inspiration and guidance, if those are terms which can be used in respect to a she-wolf and her vicious whelps.

A theme that repeats itself with great frequency in the Barker-Karpis combination is the strength it derived from friendships that took root in various penitentiaries and Federal prisons. For example, Fred Barker and Karpis learned to understand and admire each other while both were imprisoned in the Kansas State Penitentiary. Karpis, allegedly dubbed "Old Creepy" because of the feeling he inspired in other mobsters with his cold, fishy stare, was smart enough to take advantage of conditions in Kansas. Convicts assigned to the coal-mines there were rewarded for extra production by having days lopped off their time, but Karpis found that working alongside him were a number of lifers.

It did not take him long to figure that for these men there was no incentive. They could, however, be stimulated into more active mining with money and such small services as he was able to render, and soon Karpis was buying the extra coal output of a half-dozen lifers and thus appreciably shortening his own sentence.

It was the kind of trick that appealed to Fred Barker, and their jail friendship was translated into a partnership on their liberation, and they committed their first murder together. It was a cowardly affair. Two days before, they had used a De Soto to pull off a robbery, and when Sheriff C. R. Kelly, of West Plains, Missouri, saw the car in a garage he recognised it as suspect. He walked over to question the occupants and was cut down by a blast of gunfire before he could draw his own weapon.

Fred Barker, Karpis, "Ma" Barker and her paramour, Arthur V. Dunlop (alias George Anderson), occupied a cottage in Thayer, Missouri, but with the murder of the sheriff they fled to St. Paul, leaving behind their latest haul. They took over a furnished house, and had not long settled in when they were joined by William Weaver, known variously as "Phoenix Donald" and "Lapland Willie." Weaver had been paroled from Oklahoma State Penitentiary, where he had been serving a life sentence for murder during a bank robbery, and where he had met "Doc" Barker and Volney Davis, jointly convicted for the slaying of a night watchman.

"Ma" Barker and Karpis were satisfied with Weaver's credentials, but although the gang lived quietly, and as inconspicuously as possible, it was noticed that whenever they left the house together one of them carried a violin case. All five knew how to play the instrument inside, but it didn't make them musicians!

It was uncanny the way the Barker-Karpis gang, throughout its lifetime, was able to smell danger before it was too late. When the St. Paul police raided their hide-out early one morning it was to find an empty house. It had been a hasty departure, and for some reason we were never able to discover they decided that Arthur Dunlop was a squealer. The day after the gang left St. Paul Dunlop's nude, bullet-riddled body was found on the shores of a lake near Webster, Wisconsin. Close by was a woman's blood-stained glove.

Kansas City was the next stop, and here the gang was reinforced by the addition of Thomas Holden and a fellow mobster, both of whom had escaped from Leavenworth; Harvey Bailey, a notorious bank robber; Larry DeVol and Bernard Phillips, a renegade policeman turned bank bandit. In June a bank at Fort Scott fell to the gang and some of the loot was used to stage an elaborate "Welcome Home" party for a classmate of Fred Barker at Kansas State Penitentiary.

The celebrations had not long been over when late in the afternoon of July 7th, 1932, F.B.I. special agents stepped out from some bushes surrounding the Old Mission Golf Course and put the bracelets on Holden, Bailey and another gangster. The other member of the foursome, Bernard Phillips, happened to be absent when these arrests took place and went streaking with the news to "Ma" Barker. The gang took off in such haste for St. Paul that a raiding party found they had left their quarters just as dinner was about to be served!

St. Paul once more—and another murder! It stemmed from the arrest of Harvey Bailey, who was tried for participation in the Fort Scott bank robbery He was defended by J. Earl Smith, a criminal attorney of Tulsa, Oklahoma, but the evidence against him was too strong and he was convicted. Shortly afterwards a mysterious telephone call lured Attorney Smith to the vicinity of the lonely Indian Hills Country Club, fourteen miles north of Tulsa. The following morning Smith's body was found, full of bullet holes.

To offset casualties that occurred for one reason or another the gang was ever on the look-out for new recruits, but they had to measure up to tough requirements. During the next few weeks two newcomers were roped in, Earl Christman, confidence man wanted in several states, and Frank Nash, who had slipped out of Leavenworth. Christman brought his moll with him. They took part in an audacious daylight raid on the Cloud County Bank at Concordia, Kansas, that yielded over 240,000 dollars.

With all this coin to play with, the Barker-Karpis organisation turned to the task of springing some of its old hands now tucked away. It was successful in getting "Doc" Barker paroled from the Oklahoma State Penitentiary and in securing from the same institution an incomprehensible "two years leave of absence" for Volney Davis. An attempt to secure the release of Lloyd Barker, another brother, doing twenty-five years in Leavenworth for mail robbery, failed.

Looking for Christmas money the gang descended on Minneapolis and murdered three in taking the Third North-Western Bank for a heavy score. Two policemen who got in their way were chopped down by machine-gun fire, and, as they were about to leave, one of the Barker-Karpis mob thought a civilian was trying to memorise the licence number of their automobile. He too died from a stream of hot lead.

It was in Reno, Nevada, that the gang holed up to enjoy the stolen money, and while there Volney Davis made a trip to Missouri to pick up his favourite moll, who had escaped from a Mid-Western penitentiary. She stayed with Davis when the mob shifted its headquarters first to St. Paul and in April of the following year to Chicago, from which city they struck successfully at the Fairbury National Bank, Fairbury, Nebraska.

In this raid, however, Earl Christman was so badly wounded that he was rushed to the home of Verne Miller. He died despite medical care and one night was secretly buried. Christman's mother wanted to know where her son's body rested, but nobody would tell her.

It was about this time that Fred Barker began to yearn for a mate and found one in the widow of a well-known bank robber killed while following his "profession." She had a history that satisfied even "Ma" Barker.

Either Christman's death or a belief that it had got into a rut persuaded the gang that new ideas were needed, and a fling was taken at kidnapping. The first victim was William A. Hamm, junior, of the Hamm Brewing Company, St. Paul. The ransom collected was 100,000 dollars, and those who played the principal parts in the snatch were Fred and "Doc" Barker, Karpis, Charles J. Fitzgerald and a widely known underworld character—Fred Goetz, alias "Shotgun Zeigler," purportedly a former engineering student and football star at a Mid-Western university.

Wherever the gang moved it cast a shadow of murder, and two further slayings were added in quick succession to the lengthening list. In a stick-up of the Stockyards National Bank, South St. Paul, a police officer was killed outright and another crippled for life; the loot was 30,000 dollars. In Chicago the mob pounced on two bank messengers, but again they got very little, and in fleeing became involved in a minor mishap with their car. Unaware of the robbery which had taken place only a few minutes earlier, Patrolman Miles

A. Cunningham approached the bandit car at an intersection on Jackson Boulevard to inquire into the accident. Without warning he was blasted to death with a machine-gun.

By the end of the year the mob, now idling in Reno again, was more motley than ever. "Ma" Barker was there and so, too, was Fred, with the widow of the bank robber, who still stuck to him. A seasoned shoplifter had teamed up with William Weaver and Karpis, Volney Davis and Fred Goetz had their molls with them. Towards the end of the year all of them set out for St. Paul. They had planned to rob the Commercial State Bank, but on the way they got another idea. Instead of a hold-up—the danger was great and the reward uncertain—why not snatch the bank president, Edward George Brenner? The task would be much easier and it would open the bank vaults for whatever sum they demanded.

On the night of January 13th the gang gathered at the apartment of William Weaver and his paramour for a final checkup. Everything had been worked out, and those who were to do the job were soon able to leave. But as they drew away from the kerb another car, containing several men, one of them in uniform, fell in behind them. One of the bandits yelled "It's the cops" and instantly guns began to blaze. The bandit car sped away at last, leaving behind two badly wounded employees of Northwest Airways—the "cops" the gang thought they had spotted.

This fiasco did not upset the original plan, it only delayed it, and four days later five members of the Barker-Karpis outfit "took" Brenner as he halted his car at a street signal after dropping his nine-year-old daughter at a private school. There followed almost a month of complicated negotiations, with the F.B.I. keeping close watch but deferring to the family wish to effect the bank president's release before taking action. The gang collected 200,000 dollars in five- and ten-dollar bills. Brenner was then released in the vicinity of Rochester, Minnesota.

It was at this juncture that things began to get complicated for the gang. Fred Goetz offended some of his gangland pals and was executed by two blasts from a shotgun which blew off his face. There is no evidence to show if it was the vengeance of the Barker-Karpis mob, but it was certainly effective! Soon the strain of associating with the mob—their unbridled violence and the frenzy of escaping from one hide-out to another to avoid the special agents they knew were hunting them—proved too much for Goetz's moll. She became deranged and was placed in an asylum.

Converting the hot Hamm and Brenner snatch money to clean bills was a problem far from easy to solve, and the tortuous negotiations and fixing that were required almost transcend belief.

First to offer assistance was a suspect Chicago politician and ward heeler known as "Boss" McLaughlin. He was not too bright, though, and our special agents picked him up in quick time. His wife telegraphed both the President of the United States and the Attorney-General protesting against his arrest. Nevertheless, McLaughlin stayed in jail.

Next to be recruited to handle the hot money was a certain Dr. Joseph P. Moran, who had once served time for abortion and of late had looked after any hood who needed his services. In turn Dr. Moran got his nephew to help him, and apparently the arrangement was that Dr. Moran would get hold of enough of the ransom funds to put his nephew through medical school!

Yet a third character emerged in the negotiations. He was a fifty-year-old Chicago gambler with connections reaching all the way to Havana. He managed to exchange nearly 100,000 dollars of the tainted money for Cuban gold, which a well-known bank then converted into one-thousand-dollar American bills at a discount of a quarter of one per cent!

During this time Dr. Moran (he was to disappear later, and according to reliable underworld reports his weighted body was dumped by his "pals" into Lake Erie) operated on Fred Barker and Alvin Karpis in an attempt to obliterate their fingerprints and change their looks. Both realised time was running out, but what they suffered on the operating table did no good. They could not hide their identity as public enemies; they nor other members of the gang for whom there was no escape from justice.

Volney Davis, "Doc" Barker and Harry Campbell also underwent the agonisingly painful Moran "refresher" treatment to no avail. The gang did not stay in one place long. They doubled back on their tracks, dodged to this city and that county, but they could not throw off the pursuit of F.B.I. agents and decided to split up into small units. They then scattered to locations as widely separated as Glasgow (Montana), Allandale (Florida), Las Vegas, Miami, Cleveland and Havana. It was the beginning of the end.

On the night of January 8th, 1935, special agents arrested "Doc" Barker in Chicago. He was traced through a woman with whom he had become infatuated. When the apartment of the couple was searched a sub-machine-gun was found which had been stolen from a guard at the time of the St. Paul payroll robbery.

The same night special agents surrounded the apartment occupied by Russell Gibson and another mobster and their girl friends. Ordered to surrender, all but Gibson complied. Armed with a Browning and a Colt automatic he tried to get out through a rear door, but it was being watched. Gibson fired and missed, and that was the end of him. As his body was carted to the morgue the F.B.I. were collecting a small arsenal inside the apartment.

Oddly enough, it was an alligator which put the finger on "Ma" and Fred Barker! In "Doc" Barker's apartment agents found a map of Florida and a circle round Ocala and Lake Weir. Earlier they had been tipped off that mother and son were hiding out in some southern area that sheltered an ancient alligator known to the natives as "Old Joe." Now they knew for certain, and at five-thirty on a crisp January morning, with the mists hanging over Lake Weir, a picked group of special agents surrounded a cottage on the shore in which "Ma" Barker and her son were holed up.

"We are special agents of the Federal Bureau of Investigation," called out the leader. "I'm talking to you, Kate Barker, and you, Fred Barker. Come out one at a time and with your hands up!"

Further commands were issued, but in the cottage all was silent. The minutes ticked by, and once again the Barkers were ordered to come out singly, unless they wanted to be driven out by tear gas and any other means deemed necessary.

After fifteen minutes "Ma" Barker shouted: "All right, go ahead!" For a moment it looked as if mother and son had decided to throw in their hands, but then a machine-gun began to speak from the house and it swept the surrounding trees and tore into the undergrowth. It sparked off a battle that went on for hours. Tear-gas bombs were tossed into the cottage and a deadly fire from automatics was concentrated on the firing points within. It was a fight to a deadly finish, and when the F.B.I. were at last able to enter the cottage they found "Ma" Barker dead, still grasping a machine-gun in her left hand. Fred was doubled over in death, a .45 Colt automatic beside his stiffening body.

There was enough ironware in the cottage to keep a regiment at bay; two Thompson sub-machine-guns, Browning .12 gauge shot-gun, Remington shotgun, two .45 automatics, two Winchester rifles and a .38 Colt automatic, along with machine-gun drums, automatic-pistol clips and ammunition for every weapon.

There was a letter, too, from "Doc" Barker, in which he wrote: "I took care of that business for you boys. It was done just as good as if you had did it yourself. I am just like Standard Oil—always at your service. Ha, ha!"

"That business" referred to by "Doc" was, as to be expected, a slight case of murder! The victim, if such a term can be used, was William J. Harrison, who had moved within the orbit of the Capone syndicate before he joined the Barker-Karpis mob. Later his relia-bility became suspect, and from his Florida hole Fred Barker had ordered Harrison's execution. "Doc" Barker had seen to it. They took Harrison to an abandoned barn near Ontarioville in Illinois on a wild, dark night and shot him. The body, and the barn itself, was then saturated with paraffin and a match was tossed in.

As the F.B.I. ring narrowed, Alvin Karpis and Harry Campbell, with their women, scuttled from Miami to Atlantic City. There a gun battle with the police took place and Karpis and his crony came temporarily to rest in Toledo, Ohio. Meanwhile, Volney Davis was picked up by special agents in St. Louis. He was found to be carrying a counterfeit hundred-dollar bill, and was quick to explain that he "wasn't shoving the queer." He carried the bill with him, he said, to offer as a bribe should he be arrested by law-enforcement officers!

One of the gang surrendered in Kansas after a gun fight, and then William Weaver and his moll were cornered and captured in a house in Allandale, Florida. Although the Barker-Karpis organisa-tion had not merely been split open but virtually destroyed, Karpis and Campbell still had some fight left in them, as can be seen from what followed. It was so fantastic that it is hardly believable.

Karpis picked up a few hoods, among them several ex-convicts, and a gambler who must have believed in his luck. On April 24th, 1935, three heavily armed raiders pounced on a mail truck at War-ren, Ohio, and got away with 70,000 dollars and then pulled off a robbery worth 30,000 dollars against the Erie train—Detroit to

Pittsburgh. Introduced was a new tactic in robbery—the thieves escaped by aeroplane.

These exploits were followed by an alliance that only a script writer could dream up. Karpis and his crony fled to Hot Springs, Arkansas, where they were afforded protection by the chief of police and the chief of detectives. While an F.B.I. "wanted" poster for leaders of the mob aged and yellowed in the very centre of the jail door at Hot Springs, Karpis and his pals roamed at will through the streets of the spa. Nor was that all, for Karpis bedded up with an adroit woman who not only kept him happy, but also one of the law-enforcement officers as well. She divided her time between the two and owed her vast experience to the fact that she had begun operating brothels at the age of seventeen.

Eventually Hot Springs became a little too warm for Karpis. He was well aware he was being hunted, and in the early part of 1936 he again got on the move. With him was a crony who brought his girl along—a twenty-one-year-old prostitute. This time Karpis's destination was New Orleans, and although he may have thought he had again slipped the net it was in that city he had a rendezvous with justice!

Evil and merciless, Karpis had dealt out so much death that he had every reason to declare, as he had often done, that he would never be taken alive. We knew he was a problem, and planned the raid carefully. It was approximately five-fifteen in the afternoon of May 1st, 1936. Four assistants and myself were to enter by the front door. Other squads were deployed at each side of the building and at the rear. We were about to move in when a man on a horse moved into the lane beside the through traffic.

We waited, anxious to avoid attention, until the horseman had passed down the street. Now was the time for action, but then two men stepped from the doorway and walked briskly down the steps. We recognised Alvin Karpis and his crony. As they made their way towards their car, a little boy on a bicycle scooted between the pair and our vantage-point. We did not want the child hurt, as he might be if shooting started at that moment, so we moved out and hurried forward, calling for the surrender of the fugitives as they were getting into the car.

Perhaps Karpis had come to believe in his own indestructibility. I am sure he had never expected to meet the top G-man and a squad of what he had been pleased to call "sissy" agents. His expression was divided between amazement and fright and his colour was ashen. Neither he nor his shaking companion raised as much as a finger. There was no gunplay, not the remotest chance of any. Like all their breed they derived their courage from getting the drop on their victims. When they were on the wrong end of a gun the fight went out of them—as it does with every hoodlum, who is a coward at heart. Karpis told me that he thought he would never be taken alive—but then Karpis did not know Karpis.

Six days after his arrest we picked up the rest of the gang in Toledo. It was the end of an era of violence.

The Peeping-Tom Murders

by Mattias Eynck, Chief of the North Rhine-
Westphalia Murder Squad, Düsseldorf, Germany

I AM AWARE that criminologists regard multiple killers as fascinating subjects for study, and I too, perhaps, could become just as engrossed in their warped minds if I were in a position to regard murder with something like academic detachment. But as the chief of a murder squad, whose job it is to put killers into the hands of justice with as little delay as possible, I can testify there is no greater nightmare than that of hunting a killer in the grip of blood-lust. Such a person is entirely different from the murderer who has killed only once. He is neither haunted nor terrorised by his deeds, and with every fresh slaying he becomes more daring and self-assured and more cunning. He sees himself not as Fate's instrument, as do some killers, but as arbiter and destroyer in his own right. While he is at liberty nobody is safe.

The man who killed five people in and around Düsseldorf in a little over three months in the early part of 1956 possessed these grandiose ideas to dictate death to others. His first victim was a well-known business-man named Dr. Servé, who was shot dead in his car in a secluded spot on the right bank of the Rhine. The bullet, a .9 mm. revolver, tore an ugly wound in his head and pierced the brain.

Dr. Servé was not alone when he was killed. He had with him a companion, a young man, who was found unconscious in the car. He had been bludgeoned and was taken to hospital in a critical condition. He recovered, however, and told the police at his bedside what had taken place.

"Dr. Servé and I were sitting in the car discussing business when a man jerked open the door to the driving seat and shot Dr. Servé through the head. There was another person with the killer and I saw him spring forward and open the door on my side. He told me to crouch down if I wanted to save my life. He then hit me over the head with something hard. Everything happened very quickly, but before I lost consciousness I heard my assailant say to the other man, 'He won't wake again,' or something like that. It is all I can remember."

"Can you describe the two men?" asked a police officer.

The young man, bandaged and pale, said he could not. It was getting towards dusk and they were taken by surprise. The murder and the assault occurred almost simultaneously.

This brief explanation was all we had to work on. The car was examined for fingerprints, but there was nothing doing, and it seemed likely that the killer and his confederate had worn gloves to protect themselves. A careful search was made for the murder weapon, but if it had been thrown away it was not to be found.

In my office on the third floor of the Düsseldorf Präsidium of Police I studied the reports of the detectives engaged on the inquiry. Robbery, it seemed, was the motive for the murder, for Dr. Servé's wallet had been stolen. The killing had been quite ruthless and the victim had not even been given the chance of handing over his money. The accessory was obviously the weaker character. Rather than murder Dr. Servé's companion he had knocked him unconscious and pretended he had killed him. It was a very queer set-up.

"Lonely spot" murders always present special problems. The killer is a ghost not always to be laid by patience and diligence, and our investigation had run aground when yet another crime, even more fiendish than the slaying of Dr. Servé, took place. The victims were Herr Falkenberg and Fräulein Wassing, and their charred bodies were found beneath the ashes of what had been a great pyre of straw. Falkenberg had been shot through the mouth with a small-calibre revolver and his head crushed in, presumably with the butt. Laboratory tests on the body of the girl showed that she had been given an injection of cyanide.

The newspapers at once began to ask if the two crimes were not the work of the same killer, as indeed it seemed. It was undeniable that there were points of similarity between them, and, unfortunately, this theory could be extended to our investigation. We were baffled as much by one case as the other. It was not that our inquiries were less exhaustive than was reasonably possible, but that the few facts available in each case just died on us.

The wiseacres were still shaking their heads when a third crime took place. It had the same grisly mien as its predecessors, but if it was not less mystifying, at least it confirmed that the killer among us had become emboldened by success and that there was a pattern to his crimes.

His newest victims were a certain Herr Behre and a Fräulein Kuessmann. The attack on them took place not long after they had stopped their car on a lonely stretch of road outside Düsseldorf to have a little cuddle. They were battered into insensibility and their car pushed into a deep pool, where they were drowned.

At a conference at police headquarters to discuss a new approach to these crimes, a red circle on a map of the city and its environs showed the area in which the unknown killer had operated during the last few months.

"There is a view in some quarters that this man is a raving lunatic who kills at the height of his frenzies," I said to the detectives who had searched in vain for some trace of him. "I don't share this opinion. He's a killer and absolutely merciless, but I believe that he is clever and has a lot of nerve. To lay him by the heels one has to be smarter than he is."

I realised that this and other comments I felt bound to make were hardly likely to endear me to my colleagues, but we were all under some strain. The killer was our responsibility and none of us would sleep other than uneasily until he was caught.

"It is quite possible," I said, trying to be conciliatory, "that he will be taken before he commits his next murder."

And that, to everybody's infinite relief, is precisely what happened, and in this way. In the late evening of June 6th, shortly after the sun had gone down and shadows lengthened over the city and countryside, the chief forester for Büderich, a pretty village six and a half kilometres from Düsseldorf and where cheeses are made, was patrolling a nearby wood. The forester's name was Spath and he had a good eye and a quiet approach, which was just as well, for suddenly he came on a scene across which lay the shadow of impending murder. Blind to their danger, a couple sat embracing in their parked car as a man crept towards them gripping a small revolver in his right hand. Without a thought for his own safety Spath ran forward and the gunman then promptly fled, tossing his gun into a bush. The chief forester raced after him, and after a brief chase caught up with him, crouching, breathless, in a hollow.

"What's your little game?" asked Spath.

"Nothing. I was just taking a walk through the woods."

"Yes, with a gun in your hand. You were sneaking up on a parked car and I am going to arrest you."

In his official capacity Spath possessed this authority and he took his quarry to the local police station. The woods prowler gave his name as Werner Boost, aged twenty-eight, married and the father of two children. He said he was employed as a mechanic by a firm of engineers in Düsseldorf.

The gun he had thrown away was recovered and he was charged with illegally possessing a firearm and with stealing a motor-cycle. He was sentenced to six months' imprisonment and immediately appealed against the conviction.

These were, of course, minor charges, in which I was not greatly interested. It was the testimony of Chief Forester Spath that was important. Much more was known about the man who had crept up on a courting couple than was revealed in the police court.

Werner Boost had a bad record. He had begun stealing at the age of six and had spent the greater part of the war in a penal institution for young delinquents near Magdeburg, which now is, of course, in the Russian zone of East Germany. He was released for military service some little time before the war ended and at the capitulation was taken prisoner by the British, but set free within two months.

In 1951 Boost was sentenced in Düsseldorf to nine months for robbing cemeteries of urns and other metal containers, which he sold at high prices for scrap. The judge who tried him in passing sentence declared: "The accused is a man without any human feeling and is capable of anything."

Later, Boost was fined for possessing firearms without a police permit. He was not always in regular employment and had drifted from one job to another, usually with engineering firms.

I had him brought to my office, because there were a lot of questions I wanted to ask him, and which I was entitled to put to him according to German law. Boost was dark and very good-looking. He was supremely confident of himself, even arrogant, and throughout the interview there was not a single occasion when he grew abashed.

"You're a very lucky man, Herr Boost," I said to him when he was seated before my desk.

"In what way am I lucky?" he replied with a hard stare. "You know that I am appealing against my sentence."

"Had it not been for the timely intervention of Chief Forester Spath, you might well have been charged with a much more serious offence."

Boost did not reply. He sat very upright, his hands in his pockets, and with his eyes boring into mine.

"Tell me, Herr Boost," I asked, "do you usually carry a revolver with you when you go walking in the woods?"

"Sometimes."

"Would you like to explain?"

"I'm keen on shooting. As a matter of fact, I'm something of a crack shot. I take my pistol with because I like to have a little target practice."

"What sort of target practice do you prefer? Shooting at people, for example?"

His mouth became, so it appeared, a tight red scar. "What do you mean?" he asked angrily. "What are you trying to infer?"

"You were going to shoot that couple in the car. Spath saw you creeping towards them with a revolver in your hand."

"That's a lie," said Boost coldly, and then paused. "Not about the revolver, of course—I admit I was carrying it—but what you say about my going to shoot the couple. I was merely going to scare them."

"Perhaps you would like to tell me why you wanted to scare them."

He sucked in his breath and said: "It angers me whenever I see a man with a girl in a parked car in some lonely place. Nine times out of ten, he's just a bloody capitalist who wants to abuse some nice girl who is stupid enough to trust him. Or else it's some good-time secretary who imagines she can put the screw on her boss by letting him maul her about. It's beastly! It makes me see red."

"You have no permit to carry firearms," I reminded him.

"No. I did not think it necessary for a little harmless target practice."

"Or frightening couples in cars?"

"I consider I am doing the community a service. These sex horrors are the curse of Germany."

"Doctor Servé was not with a girl," I said after a short silence. "Or did you think he was?"

"What has Dr. Servé got to do with me? He was murdered, wasn't he? Are you trying to fix the crime on me simply because you can't discover the real culprit. Herr Eynck, you are barking up the wrong tree. The murder of Dr. Servé is your headache, not mine. Let us be quite clear about it."

It was something for him to think about, and, in any case, I had another question for him. "Who is Franz Lorbach?" I asked.

Boost frowned and I took a little diary from my drawer and said: "This was found in the saddle-bag of your motor-cycle." I flipped over the pages to one marked with a slip of paper and read: "Sunday, June 3rd, 'Lorbach seems in need of another shot. Must attend to it.' Be good enough to explain what it means."

"It's easy to explain. Franz Lorbach is a friend of mine and we are both keen on shooting. The last occasion we tested our marksmanship—it was on Sunday, June 3rd—he was badly off the mark. He just couldn't get a bull's-eye. So I made a note to give him another shot. I like to try my skill against a worthy opponent."

"You're a plausible liar," I mused, but I did not argue further with him at this stage.

As I replaced the diary in the drawer I remembered something that my mind had pigeon-holed at the time I had first read Boost's dossier. Let me explain that in the autumn of 1945, when the war had not long been over, the authorities at Helmstedt, a medieval town between the Russian and British occupation zones, had reported that about fifty persons had been killed in trying to cross the border to the British zone. It had not been possible to account for the murders, and, in fact, nobody had greatly troubled about them. The victims, the driftwood of war, took a chance in trying to get over, and if they failed it was just too bad. Anyhow, what interested me most was that Boost, according to his dossier, had been in Helmstedt at the time these murders took place. He had gone there after the British had released him, to try and earn some easy money as a guide to those trying to cross the border. There was nothing to link him with the killings, but it struck me that it was not without significance that they had ceased when he left the area and returned to Düsseldorf.

"When you were in Helmstedt in 1945 did you ever indulge in a little target practice by shooting refugees crossing the border from the Russian zone?"

It was, of course, a random shot, but Boost remained undisturbed.

"Gott in Himmel!" he said. "Certainly not! I was only too eager to help the poor devils. You must be mad, Herr Eynck."

"You like shooting, but you don't shoot to kill, is that it?"

He looked at me with an expression which told me he would dearly have liked to have driven his fist into my face.

"I don't shoot people," he replied coldly. "Get that straight. I know you must be very worried over the murders that have taken place in the last few months. But you can't make me the scapegoat for them or anything else you have failed to clear up."

At that moment I got a buzz on the intercom. from my secretary.

"There's a man here by the name of Franz Lorbach. Says he wishes to see you and that it is very important."

This was, of course, Boost's friend, and I curbed my excitement and said:

"Let him wait in your room. I'll call you when I am disengaged."

Boost stared coolly at me as I put down the receiver and said to him: "That will be all for the present. You seem to have given fairly conclusive answers to my questions. It may be necessary to see you again later. In the meantime, you will be returned to prison until your appeal is heard."

Summoning the officer who had waited outside the door, I handed Werner Boost over, then called through the intercom. for Franz Lorbach to be shown in.

He was a pleasant, rather frail-looking man, as timid as the other was bold. His face was pale, and his eyes watery and he had a weak chin. His nose twitched like that of a rabbit. He looked nervous enough to be a drug-taker. His gaze ran round the room as he took the chair I offered, as though to make certain we were alone.

Then he said in a thin, nervous voice: "It is very good of you to see me, Herr Eynck. What I have to say is important, most important."

"Go on," I encouraged. "You can speak quite freely here. There are no hidden microphones or tape recorders."

He returned my smile wanly, flicked the tip of his nose with a bony index finger, and went on: "I had to see you, Herr Eynck, because I want to tell you all I know about Werner Boost, the man they arrested in Büderich woods. He is a killer, a murderer of the worst kind. I am frightened, Herr Eynck, very frightened. You must protect me."

"There's no need to be frightened, Lorbach," I replied. "We won't let any harm come to you, be sure of that. Just tell me plainly and simply all you wish to say."

He swallowed several times, as though to rid himself of a lump in his throat.

"He's a monster, an ogre," he went on, wringing his hands. "I'm in his power; hypnotised by him. He forces me to do things I don't want to. If only I could get free from his evil spell."

"Calm down," I remonstrated, "and please, no dramatics. Just start at the beginning. How long have you known Boost and how did you first meet up with him?"

"I first met him in 1952," said Lorbach. "I was a gamekeeper on a large estate near Büderich. I had a liking for poaching and that is how I formed a friendship with Boost. We chummed up in the woods one evening. I was a good shot and so was he. This love of shooting drew us together. After that, we often met and went poaching. It was during these meetings that I discovered he had one great obsession. He hated to see courting couples in the woods. Sometimes he would spy on them to watch what they were up to. Whenever he saw a couple petting in a car he became excited. 'Watch me, Franz,' he would murmur. 'I'll give them the works.' And he would creep up to the car and surprise the occupants."

"Did he ever use a gun?" I asked.

"Yes, often. He would threaten to shoot them dead unless the man paid him money. He got away with it time after time. Naturally, the couples did not report him. People are never keen to disclose such matters to the police, especially if they are having a clandestine affair. Believe me, Boost obtained plenty of cash from these adventures."

"Did he give you any of it?"

"Yes. At first I merely kept watch while he did the threatening. Later I took a more active part."

"In what way?"

"Well, you see, Boost had a good knowledge of chemistry. He fixed up a small laboratory in the cellar of his home. He was always reading textbooks on the subject which he borrowed from the library. He prepared a concoction which stupefied the couples he surprised in their cars. After robbing the men, he gratified his lust with the unconscious women. And I took part in it too. Some of the girls were very lovely. I cannot think why I did it. I have a wife of my own." Lorbach covered his face. "She is going to have a baby," he said. "I have been a beast. But it was Boost who made me do these vile things. He goaded me, called me a silly, sensitive coward if I hesitated. Oh God! How easily I let myself be drawn into his clutches."

"What else?" I asked, for it was evident Franz Lorbach had more to tell.

"That is how things were, Boost the master, me the willing accomplice, until that frightful evening last January."

"You mean the evening when Dr. Servé was murdered?" I asked.

"Yes. We were walking along the Rhine bank intending to shoot a few rabbits. He had been telling me of a devilish device he had thought up for killing couples without shooting them. 'I know you cannot bear the sight of blood, you squeamish idiot,' he sneered.

"His idea was to fill some toy balloons with cyanide gas which he said he could make by heating a mixture of cyanide of potassium with acid. It would then be easy to creep up to a parked car containing a spooning couple, push the nozzle of the balloon through the window and then release the gas. The couple would become insensible immediately and easy victims for robbery. 'If the fumes kill them, what odds?' he exclaimed. 'That kind are better out of the way. Their dirty minds and their love of sex are a disgrace to the country.' "

Lorbach broke off.

"Tell me about Dr. Servé," I said.

He closed his eyes. "Dr. Servé," he repeated. "Ah, yes. That was shocking. I had a feeling something terrible was going to happen. As we walked along and Boost talked about his plan with the cyanide

gas, we suddenly noticed a large expensive car drawn up in a secluded spot. 'Look!' he cried. 'There's another bloody capitalist
taking advantage of a girl. Here goes! I'll teach him a lesson he
won't forget in a hurry. Come on.' He pulled out his revolver, holding it at the ready, and went stealthily forward just as one sees cow-
boys do in a Western film.

"When he got up to the car, he pulled the door open and fired his
revolver straight at the man in the driver's seat. I saw the man's
blood spatter over the windscreen as he fell forward over the wheel,
and it turned me sick. Acting on impulse, I darted to the other
door of the car and got it open. The other person inside was not
a girl, as I had expected, but a young man. Boost yelled at me to
kill him, but I couldn't. This was murder, horrible cold-blooded
murder. I just couldn't kill for the sake of killing.

"I whispered to the young man to crouch down in his seat while
I hit him over the head and to sham death if he wanted to save his
life. He understood me, and I hit him with the butt of my own pistol.
'He won't wake up again,' I cried to Boost. He became very angry
and called me a cowardly rat, but calmed down when he saw the
young fellow slumped in the car. 'I hope you've made a proper job
of him,' he said. 'I'll bet they were here for no good, sitting together
in a car in a spot like this. Now let's see what they've got of any
value.'

"Boost took the dead man's wallet from his jacket. It contained
a fair amount of money. The young man had nothing of any value
on him. As we went away, I felt frightfully ill and started retching.
Boost gave me some tablets to swallow. 'They will help you,' he
said. As the tablets began to work, I felt as if I had no will left,
but the feeling of nausea had gone.

"The next day I was too ill to get up. Boost called on me early
and ordered me to get out of bed and go to work, otherwise my
absence might give rise to suspicion, he said.

"In spite of feeling rotten I did as he told me. That evening he
gave me more tablets. Later he started giving me injections. I believe the stuff was morphia. That is how he has kept me in his
power. I am a tool in his hands."

"Why have you not come to the police and told all this before?"
I asked.

Lorbach stared at me, as if the question really needed no answer.

"I was too frightened," he confessed. "I was sure Boost would kill me. He is a callous, vindictive man. To him, killing a human being is no different to slaughtering an animal. Had I squealed he would have murdered me as surely as he murdered the others. I was afraid, too, that the police might not believe such a fantastic story and would have me put away in an asylum. I did go to the priest once and asked him if it would be a crime to commit justifiable homicide in order to stop an habitual murderer from continuing to take life. The priest smiled and asked me what was on my mind. I came away. How could I tell him?"

I arrested Franz Lorbach as an accessory to the murder of Dr. Servé and he made a full statement. It filled no less than 370 pages and provided further details of his association with Boost.

His confederate, he declared, ordered him to shoot a woman who fetched the pay for a factory staff from a bank every Friday. The robbery was carefully planned and rehearsed, but at the last minute Lorbach said he could not go through with it and willingly gave Boost 600 marks (roughly £50) as compensation.

"It was at that time," said Lorbach, "that I received eight thousand marks (about £660) from a legacy and which I placed in a savings bank. Gradually it has dwindled away until now there is hardly any of it left. I have been obliged to part with most of the money to Boost to compensate him for my failure to carry out crimes he ordered me to commit. Had it not been for the injections he insisted on giving me, I could not have kept going at all."

Werner Boost schemed to rob a savings bank at Oberkassel, near Bonn, and shoot up everyone inside. Lorbach prevented this by pretending that an elderly man sitting on a bench outside the building was his uncle and had recognised him. So the plan was dropped.

Soon additional evidence began to pile up. A ballistics expert proved beyond any doubt that the revolver Boost threw away the evening Chief Forester Spath chased him was the very weapon with which Dr. Servé was shot.

We searched Boost's home and found the laboratory in the cellar. It contained a large stock of chemicals, including cyanide of potassium. In a cardboard box were several toy balloons.

Acting on further information supplied by Lorbach, detectives discovered, buried in a wood at Merebusch and in a cemetery near

Büderich, a quantity of jewellery, watches and other valuables Boost is believed to have stolen from his victims.

At my request, the police of Lower Saxony have reopened investigations into the 1954 murders on the zonal border around Helmstedt.

Meanwhile, Boost remains in custody while the North Rhine-Westphalia police proceed to make the case against him watertight. When completed, the indictment will be one of the longest on record.

If the charges are proved, and there seems little doubt of that, Werner Boost will go to prison for life. In Germany there is no death penalty for murder.

The Tell-Tale "Dabs"

by Ex-Chief Superintendent Frederick Cherrill,
formerly in charge of Scotland Yard's
Fingerprint Bureau, London

A CCORDING to the form book, the killer of Mrs. Freeman Lee, the ninety-four-year-old recluse whose body was found in a black leather trunk in the hall of her decayed house in Maidenhead, would have been declared, by ordinary reckoning, a nonrunner; but occasionally, as in racing, one can throw away the form book and really come up with a surprise result—the long shot no one has expected. It was so in this case, for the old woman, who had lived among cobwebs and memories for so many years, was strangled by a rank outsider, at least as judged by the pattern of behaviour known to criminologists.

He was a modest little screwsman, never known to raise his hand in anger or . . . But let me begin at the beginning of this story of a single and fragmentary clue that put the rope round his neck by saying that in my thirty-three years at Scotland Yard I do not ever remember a case as fascinating—I mean, of course, a fingerprint case.

A couple of untouched milk bottles on the doorstep led to the discovery of the murder on June 1st, 1948. Mrs. Freeman Lee lived in an old Victorian house called Wynford in Ray Park Avenue, Maidenhead. She had been battered over the head and strangled, and when her body was pulled out of the five-foot trunk it was found that she had been gagged and her arms tied behind her back with a bed-jacket.

The Chief Constable of Berkshire asked Scotland Yard for help, and assigned to the case were the late Chief Superintendent William Chapman, head of the Flying Squad, and Detective-Sergeant David Hislop. They found that Mrs. Freeman Lee was known in the neighbourhood as an eccentric. She was the widow of a barrister of some means and had had her share of ill luck. Her only son was killed in the first world war, and when her husband died a few years later, Mrs. Freeman Lee became a recluse. She was then sixty-nine. Her friends saw her no longer and she seldom went out. The big house, in which she had been mistress for over forty years, and where many gay parties had taken place, became more derelict every year, for she occupied only one of the rooms on the ground floor. There she cooked and, perhaps, did a little sewing, and spent her days and nights alone and isolated.

Very occasionally she was seen in Maidenhead in clothes that fashion had long forgotten, and those who remembered her would point to her as the old woman who did not know how much she was worth and lived in a great house whose riches—carpets, tapestries, paintings and heaven knows what else—had become musty with neglect. That was what gossip did for an old woman who long ago had retreated to within herself.

Scotland Yard has a Fingerprint Bureau of a million sets of "dabs," as we call them. They are so expertly classified that whenever a crime investigation yields a set it is not unusual for them to be identified within a few minutes. That is, of course, if they are the prints of somebody with a criminal record.

When I went down to Maidenhead, as chief of the Bureau, it was to search for any marks the murderer might have left behind. The house in Ray Park Avenue was a page out of Dickens—windows which had never been opened, rooms that belonged to forgotten ghosts, cornices draped in cobwebs, the smell of mildew and dry rot and crumbling floors and walls. There were four great reception rooms on the ground floor, seven bedrooms on the next, four on the second floor and two attics overhead, but none had been used for years, except a front room on the ground floor where the old woman had lived and died. It was the only place to look, nothing would be found elsewhere.

It was here the murderer had searched frantically for the riches the old woman was supposed to have hidden. It was full of odd and ancient pieces of furniture and he had plunged into the drawers of a hefty sideboard and a tallboy for money and jewels that were not to be found. The floor was strewn with what he had pushed out of the drawers—bits of finery, a fan; the vestiges of the past the old woman had hoarded and most likely forgotten about.

I began the examination of the furniture, every piece of it from the single and bedraggled bed to the wardrobe, sideboard, tallboy, the little table on which stood a radio set, the fine china, a bowl of fruit, a water jug and basin, a quart bottle of beer that was nearly empty, even tins of fruit stacked together. I found fingerprints all right, but they belonged to the dead woman; there was not a trace of the intruder, not a single mark that he had left. It was the same with the windows and doors and the black trunk itself, which had been the old woman's temporary coffin.

I went back into the room and began to strip the bed. The clothes were in disarray, but, as I picked up the down quilt, from its folds fell silently to the floor a tiny cardboard box. It was white and square, the kind in which trinkets are sold and kept. I got my glass on it, and although it was clear that it had been handled, there was nothing that could be described as a fingerprint. Perhaps, I thought, I shall have better luck with the lid of the little box, and I began to remove the rest of the bedclothes, but there was not a sign of it.

Now I knew that a thief would not overlook a little box of this description, and I was aware, too, that persons of the age and eccentricity of Mrs. Freeman Lee would not keep it without a lid. I wanted this little lid badly and began to look around until I realised where I might find it. Kneeling down I peered under the bed and saw the little white square of cardboard. Somebody had trodden on it, for its narrow sides, five-sixteenths of an inch exactly, were flat.

I had a pair of forceps handy and I laid the lid very gently on a sheet of paper. It bore the imprint of a firm of fancy goods and leather manufacturers in New York. Manœuvring the lid with the forceps I examined it carefully through a magnifying glass, and on the outside of the flattened edges I could just make out two faint fingermarks. They could hardly have been fainter, but I knew they did not belong to the old woman.

No jeweller ever packed a little box and its lid with greater care, and I could not get back to Scotland Yard quickly enough to have the faint marks on the lid photographed. The certainty that every fingerprint is absolutely unique and individual, and that in this respect Nature never repeats itself, is the rock on which the science of dactyloscopy is founded. No two fingerprints can ever be identical, unless made by the same finger. It is as simple as that, and as infallible, and I knew that if the person whose fingerprints were on the little square of cardboard I had picked up in that musty old bedroom in Maidenhead had a criminal record, we would find him.

When the photographs of the prints were laid on my desk I took a long look at them and decided they had been made by a right thumb and a right ring finger. It was then that I rang for my assistant, Chief Inspector Edward Holten.

"Take a look at these," I said. "Unless I'm very much mistaken they're the 'dabs' of a murderer. I found them at Maidenhead, and nothing else. Have a go, Ted, and see if you can fix them up. I am pretty sure they belong to one of our 'clients.' "

Holten took up the photographs and did not look terribly impressed. "There's not too much to go on," he said. "They look pretty thin to me."

"I fancy there's enough to swing the person who made them, if we can trace him," I replied. "See what you can do."

In less than ten minutes the chief inspector was back in my office. He carried a complete set of fingerprints from the files and I could see from the glint in his eyes that he had found what he had searched for.

He laid the prints and the file on my desk and said: "They match right enough. The name is George Russell, convicted thief and housebreaker. No fixed abode."

I studied the two sets of prints. There was no doubt that they were identical. The papillary ridges on the tip of the right ring finger matched the faint and fragmentary impressions found on the lid of the cardboard box.

"Good work, Ted," I said to Holten. "I think we can now say we know who killed Mrs. Freeman Lee."

I knew I had heard the name of George Russell somewhere as soon as Holten mentioned it, but I could not recall the circumstances until I was handed his dossier. Fifteen years before I had given evidence against him. He and a companion had broken into a public house, but actually he was arrested on another charge. His fingerprints were taken and the Oxford police had sent them to the Bureau at Scotland Yard together with a set of impressions found on the

rifled till of the public house. They tallied, and my evidence at the
Oxford Quarter Sessions was largely responsible for securing a conviction. Russell was sent to prison for this offence.

Since then, as the dossier showed, he had been "inside" on nu-
merous occasions for housebreaking, and now his "dabs" had been
picked up in a house where murder had been done.

I must say, however, that I was nagged by a single thought. Russell was no great shakes as a crook and was really small fry, but
his record showed that he was not given to using violence. Could it
be that he had broken into the house at Maidenhead with a companion who had killed the old woman while Russell searched for
the loot?

The more I thought about this theory, though, the less feasible
it became. Only Russell's "dabs" had been found, and only one room,
that occupied by the aged victim, had been entered. All the signs
indicated that the search for valuables had been done by a murderer
in a hurry. It was strictly a one-man show.

I returned to Maidenhead to tell Superintendent Chapman the
result of my findings.

"Looks as if Russell may be our man," he said when he heard
the news.

"Either that, or an accessory before and after the fact," I replied
cautiously.

The word went out from Scotland Yard that Russell was wanted
for questioning, and five days later he was picked up at St. Albans
in a hostel for tramps. Chief Superintendent Chapman asked him to
account for his movements between May 28th, when Mrs. Freeman
Lee was last seen alive, and June 1st. He gave what appeared to
be a frank explanation.

"I am a gardener by trade," he said, "and I heard that an old
lady at Wynford wanted someone to do her garden. I went there
on May 28th and took a look at the job. Seeing it in such a bad
condition, I would not entertain it. I never asked the old woman
about it, but went away and had dinner at Betty's Café. Later on,
I went into the Gardeners' Arms for a drink and got into conversation with a man named Stock and his son. I told them about
the job at Wynford, and the son said he had once worked there.
He told me I was a fool not to have done the work, because the old
lady had lots of cash."

Russell gave an account of his movements. When he left the Gardeners' Arms he went to Old Windsor and slept in a horseshed. He moved out the next morning about five-thirty and went to Staines, where he stayed the rest of the day and part of Sunday.

"On Sunday morning," he went on, "I sung hymns in the street and got some money, then I went for a trip to Brighton. I got back to London very late and stayed there that night and all the next day."

Superintendent Chapman then asked Russell if had ever entered the house of Mrs. Freeman Lee in Ray Park Avenue.

"No, never," he said without hesitation.

"You are not telling the truth," said Chapman. "Your fingerprints have been found there."

This was bad news for the suspect. He began to cry and said he wished to make a statement. He wrote it down himself, and, as will be seen from the following, which was the final paragraph of his statement, Russell did as much as anybody to convict himself.

I was told that she had a lot of money. Did I murder this poor aged woman for something she was supposed to have, but had not? I did not. I did not figure in such a murder. I am not of such a disposition. I am not prepared to risk my life by it, bad though my financial position was. I am not prepared to take the can back for someone else.

Russell was, of course, dead right about Mrs. Freeman Lee not being wealthy. However well off she may have been in the dim past, she certainly possessed no resources at the time of her murder, and, in fact, was receiving a small allowance from the benevolent fund of a legal society. But how did Russell find out that she had not the money she was supposed to have?

Chapman put the question to him sharply. "I suggest," he said, "that you found out the truth either from Mrs. Lee herself, the woman you intended to rob, or from searching her belongings after you had murdered her."

"No! No!" wailed Russell. "That is not true. Someone else killed her and you want to string me up for a crime I did not commit."

Russell was then charged with the murder of Mrs. Freeman Lee on the night of May 31st or in the early hours of June 1st and was taken to his cell sobbing and protesting.

Shortly afterwards, at a conference at Scotland Yard in connection with the preparation of the case for preliminary hearing before the magistrates at Maidenhead, Chief Superintendent Chapman said to us: "It's a rum go. Russell has got a lot of form behind him for housebreaking. Yet he's such a quiet little screwsman. Violence was never his line."

Russell unquestionably possessed a simple nature, and this was illustrated at his trial at Berkshire Assizes before Mr. Justice Hallett, rather to the discomfiture of his counsel, Mr. Eric Sachs, K.C. (now Mr. Justice Sachs).

The defence laid siege to the police evidence and Mr. Sachs drew the attention of the court to certain parts of Russell's statement, which he had signed, and suggested that it was couched in a way a policeman or detective would write, rather than a civilian.

"I proceeded here and I proceeded there," Mr. Sachs said, hitching up his gown. "Is that the sort of language the prisoner, an uneducated part thief, part vagrant, would be likely to use, or is it, as I suggest, the language of a policeman?"

It was quite an astute point and it impressed the jury, as one could see. But when Russell went into the witness-box and was invited by his counsel to describe his movements prior and up to the time of the murder, he began to use the phrase Mr. Sachs had so bitingly referred to as police talk ". . . I proceeded to the Gardeners' Arms . . . I proceeded to Old Windsor . . ." and so it went on.

The truth of it was that as a vagrant Russell had been in and out of police courts so many times that, quite unconsciously, he had formed the habit of using the same phraseology he had heard from the police officers who gave evidence against him. In this way he corroborated the testimony of Superintendent Chapman.

I think it can be said that my own evidence added to the strength of the case against Russell. I showed how the ridge characteristics in the impressions I had found on the lid of the little cardboard box matched the fingerprints of the accused.

In reply to Mr. Sachs I said: "In my thirty years' experience as a fingerprint expert, I have never known different fingers to agree in the sequence of their characteristics. Apart from those of the accused, I found no other prints save those of the dead woman."

The jury took ten minutes under two hours to reach a verdict of "Guilty," and the accused displayed no emotion as he watched the judge place the black cap on his head and say: "George Russell, after a most careful and prolonged inquiry the jury have found you guilty of an offence for which only one sentence is known to our law . . ."

The House of Lords had recently suspended the "No hanging" clause contained in the Criminal Justice Bill, passed only a few months earlier, and Russell was the first murderer to be made subject again to the old law and its formula.

His case was taken to the Court of Criminal Appeal but was dismissed, and he was hanged at Oxford Prison on December 2nd, 1948—almost twenty-one years to the day since he made his first appearance in a police court on a charge of petty larceny.

The Man
who Could Read Thoughts

by Ex-Police Chief Mike Gier, Edmonton, Alberta, and Vancouver, B.C., Canada

To RECOGNISE a killer and know that you will never be able to put him where he belongs is infuriating enough, but to be faced with a murder whose very simplicity presages defeat . . . well, that is just humiliating.

As a matter of fact the Booher case involved the slaying of not one but four persons; the tracks led everywhere and nowhere, and since the department of which I was the head was under heavy fire from various quarters, I decided that the situation called for unorthodox measures.

I knew already what people were saying about police methods, and I could guess what some of my officers were thinking when I told them what I proposed to do. Particularly Detective Jim Leslie, who was to meet the train in at Edmonton and bring Dr. Maximilian Langsner, late of Vienna, to my office.

Leslie was an astute investigator with a good record, but the Booher case had him foxed, and he had not been able to uncover a single lead that offered any hope of a solution. The slaying of four people appeared as mad and motiveless now as it did when the crime was discovered.

Let me say that I knew I might be leading with my chin in introducing Dr. Langsner to the problem. He could be a mountebank rather than the marvel some people claimed him to be.

Nevertheless, I knew of his successes elsewhere. There was, for instance, the episode at Vancouver when he had walked into police headquarters and announced that he could put the finger on the missing jewels in a robbery case which was baffling the authorities, despite the fact that they had managed to pick up a suspect.

Dr. Langsner undoubtedly had a way with him, for the police, at his suggestion, had allowed him to enter the cell of the suspect. He stood stiffly in a corner for half an hour without saying a word and then signalled to the jailer that he had finished.

To the detective in charge of the case Dr. Langsner had said: "You'll find the stolen jewels hidden behind a picture in a room whose walls are yellow."

The description did not fit the suspect's apartment, but that of his girl friend, and the detective found the jewels exactly as Dr. Langsner had depicted.

The Vancouver affair was one of three cases in which Dr. Langsner had displayed his extraordinary powers. As far as I could understand it, he had the ability to read the thoughts of others and was demonstrating this long before studies in extrasensory perception were introduced at various universities. When asked to explain his ability to tune in to another's mind he said: "It is not easy to say what happens, but there are some people who can do it."

To get back to the Booher case, Detective Leslie was hopping mad as he waited at the railway station. I knew all this, because he told me everything that happened that day—later, of course, and when he was calmer. In fact, Jim Leslie never forgot the little doctor from Vienna, and he had good reason not to, as you will see.

Dr. Langsner got off the train with an umbrella and a battered piece of luggage. Leslie stepped forward, introduced himself, and said: "Welcome to Edmonton. I am happy to meet you, and all of us are looking forward to the help we know you can give us."

There was not much of Dr. Langsner, and he appeared even smaller when he took off his hat and his hair popped out all over the place. He looked at Leslie for a moment, tapped his umbrella, and replied: "I don't believe a word you say. You would rather I hadn't come, and I know you are sure that I shall accomplish nothing. I hope, though, that we shall become friends and that I can help."

Leslie crimsoned, knowing that the doctor had read his mind. He was a good loser, though, and shrewd enough to realise at once that Dr. Langsner was no ordinary person. He asked the doctor to talk about himself, and it was not just out of politeness.

Langsner smiled and said: "I was born and educated in Vienna, and it was my good fortune to study under Freud. During the first world war I saw a lot of shell-shocked cases, and, more than ever, became interested in the mind and its functioning. In 1926 I went to India and stayed longer than I intended. I found much that surprised me in the field of intuitive control of the mind.

"It was from this experience that I learned much of what I now know. People are sceptical about my powers, but it is not my wish to be a bloodhound. I help the police whenever they ask me, or when I have a strong pull, such as I felt in the Vancouver case."

Leslie asked Langsner what had brought him to Canada, and he expained that he wanted to study the minds of the Eskimos. The Melanesians and Polynesians of the South Pacific had become indoctrinated and corrupted by Western influences, but the intuitive abilites of the Eskimos had remained unimpaired. "They sense weather changes," said Dr. Langsner with enthusiasm. "They are able to sense danger long before its appearance and they have their minds, so to speak, at their fingertips. I want to live with them and communicate with them through the channels of thought."

When Detective Leslie walked into my office with our visitor I could see that he had had a change of heart and mind. I had the feeling that Langsner did not need briefing, but I had prepared a report and began to read it and he listened without interrupting.

"On July 9th," I said, "the police at Mannville, eighty miles from here, were notified by a Dr. Heaslip that half the members of the Booher ranch had been murdered. It was evening, but the summer nights in the Arctic regions are bright and glowing and Constable Olson drove over from Mannville and found Dr. Heaslip waiting for him at the ranch house, together with the survivors, Henry Booher, his youngest son Vernon, and a neighbour, Charles Stevenson.

"Booher, middle-aged and still greatly shocked, led the way into the house. In the kitchen the body of Mrs. Booher was slumped over the table. She had died from three bullets in the back of the neck. In the next room Fred, another of the Booher sons, was sprawled on the floor. He had been shot through the mouth. A third victim was Gabriel Cromby, one of the hired hands. He was an Austrian immigrant and his body was found in the bunkhouse. Two shots had found their mark, one in the head and the other in the chest.

"Olson was unaccustomed to dealing with this type of crime, but he had the good sense to get everybody out on the porch for questioning. Vernon Booher said he had found the bodies about eight o'clock that evening. He had been working in the fields for a couple of hours and heard the shots. They seemed to come from the house, and he hurried over and found the body of his mother first. He then saw his dead brother, and when he ran over to the bunkhouse for help he discovered what had happened to Cromby. There was no telephone in the house and he got a neighbour to call Dr. Heaslip.

"The constable wanted to know if anything was missing, and Henry Booher said he thought not. His wife had a diamond ring, and it had not been taken. Vernon then remembered the other cowhand, a man named Rosyk. He had not been seen and Vernon asked if he might not be the murderer.

"The little party began to search the outhouses, and in one of the barns they found the missing man . . . Rosyk was dead from a couple of bullets. Henry Booher was asked what he had been doing at the time and if he had not heard the shots. He said: 'No, I wish to God I had heard them, but I was working too far away. There is a lot of acreage to this farm and the sounds did not carry that far.' Stevenson, the neighbour, explained his presence. He had stopped at the house to look at a farming catalogue Henry Booher had told him about. They were thinking of buying a harvester together.

"Booher corroborated this, and when asked if he had any idea who might be responsible for the murders replied:'No. As far as I can tell we have no enemies anywhere. Rose, my wife, was a well-loved woman among our community. She was always ready to help any of our neighbours.' "

I explained to Dr. Langsner that when the crime was notified to Edmonton I had sent Detective Leslie and Inspector Longacre out to the farm. "Tell the doctor what you found," I said to Leslie.

He looked a bit uncomfortable and glanced at Langsner, who was sitting very upright in his chair and grasping his umbrella.

"We carried out a routine examination, but found no strange fingerprints; just those of the Booher family and hired help. The murder weapon was a .303 rifle, but we were unable to find it.

There was a .22 rifle and an old shotgun in the house, but neither had been fired for some time. One thing that interested us was the absence of rifle shells. Whoever had done the killing had picked them up, except one, which we found in a pan of water.

"We organised a search of the countryside with the help of neighbours, but it was no good. The murder weapon is still missing, and at the moment we are stuck without a clue."

Dr. Langsner nodded sympathetically. "I can see how difficult everything is. Perhaps I shall be able to help you a little."

The inquest took place that afternoon, and Dr. Langsner occupied a seat at the Press table. Everyone wondered who he was. The inquiry did not yield much more than we knew already. Mrs. Booher was the first victim and she was killed at the table as she was preparing a dish of strawberries. Fred died next, Rosyk a little later and Cromby last of all—about two hours after the first murder.

The time factor was testified to by neighbours and other witnesses and the shots were heard between half-past six and eight o'clock in the evening. They did not arouse any concern, because around Mannville it is hunting country and almost everybody keeps a gun.

One important piece of evidence was that provided by Councilman Robert Scott, who said he had driven down the farm road about six-thirty and had stopped to talk with Vernon Booher. Rosyk put in an appearance and asked Vernon what remained to be done around the house. Vernon told him to feed the stock in the barn.

Vernon gave evidence and was asked how it was that he had not heard those shots which occurred earlier in the evening. He said that since thinking the events over he must have heard them, but had paid no attention. He knew there was a fox in the neighbourhood and that Charles Stevenson had told him that he meant bagging it.

Charles Stevenson, somewhat nervous, had not long been sworn when he was asked if he owned a gun.

"Yes, I do, but I haven't it at the moment," he said. "It has been troubling me and I want to tell you about it. My gun is a .303 and the same calibre as the murder weapon. It was in my closet, but it is not there now and I think somebody must have stolen it."

"Can you tell the court when the gun was stolen?"

"Yes. It was taken last Sunday during the time I left home to go to church. I know it was there before I left because I saw it."

"Why didn't you report the theft?"

"Aw, shucks, you know how it is round here. Neighbours just come over and borrow things if you don't happen to be around. If I wanted a gun I wouldn't think twice of taking one from the Boohers."

Henry Booher and Vernon, too, were at the church service and said that they knew nothing about the missing rifle.

Following the inquest we had a conference in my office to decide our next step, but neither Detective Leslie nor Inspector Longacre looked very happy, and that was understandable, for we had not much to work on. Nobody seemed very talkative, so to get the ball rolling I said: "It seems to me that three people could have done these murders . . . Henry Booher or Vernon or Charles Stevenson. What puzzles me most is the motive, and maybe we shall find the killing was done by a lunatic. Our first and most important task is to find the gun. It may tell us all we want to know."

Dr. Langsner was looking at me steadily and I must confess that I was half joking when I asked him: "You look as if you know something. Could it be the name of the killer?"

He was not in the mood for badinage, and like a professor addressing an inattentive class he said in a clipped voice: "The rifle is not important. There are no suspects in this case, only the murderer, and I have already recognised him."

Detective Leslie leaned forward, prepared to listen. I was not at all certain if the little doctor was not now paying me back in my own coin. Nevertheless, I asked him to name the person he thought was the killer.

"Vernon Booher," he said quite simply.

"Have you any proof?" asked Inspector Longacre.

Dr. Langsner was surprised by the question. "Of course I have no proof. How is that possible? I am sure, though, and yet I cannot tell you why I am sure. I can tell you, though, that I knew what one or two people were thinking about in court today."

"Do you mean to say you could read the minds of the witnesses as they were giving evidence?"

"I do not know if I was reading their minds, as you say, but I knew what they were thinking about."

Inspector Longacre looked very puzzled, and Dr. Langsner began to develop his theory.

"When a man commits a crime, and it may not necessarily be murder, he knows he has offended against the social code. Nevertheless, he seeks for ways to protect himself and his mind plays with the details of the crime so that he can have an explanation prepared, should it be necessary to defend himself. The problem is much more acute, naturally, when he has killed somebody, and often the persistency of thought becomes too great to bear and the criminal confesses, because only by so doing can he find relief from an intolerable burden. For instance, I know that Vernon is terribly worried by something that may prove his guilt."

"You mean the discovery of the missing rifle?" I asked. "If you know where it is, why not say so?"

Dr. Langsner sighed as if he somehow regretted our persistence. "Yes, I know where it is. When Mr. Stevenson told the court of finding that it had been taken from his home, Vernon began to think intently about the weapon. I could see where he had put it."

"And I'll bet he could, too," said Leslie quietly.

We waited for Dr. Langsner to continue. He closed his eyes and quietly said: "It is in a clump of prairie grass beyond the back of the house. It is to the west, because I can now see the sun in that direction."

Inspector Longacre gave him a hard look. He was by no means convinced that he was not a charlatan.

"I am willing to out to the farm with you," continued Langsner. "But let us go tomorrow and I will find the rifle for you. I am very tired now."

By noon next day the four of us arrived at the Booher farm. It commanded a lot of land, and the house, timbered and two-storey, was well constructed with a large veranda which the family must have used on many a summer evening when they had visitors. Everything looked well kept and spruce, and the various farm buildings stood under the shadow of some great linden trees.

I glanced once more at Dr. Langsner, and could hardly repress a chuckle. He was still carrying his umbrella on this hot day and wore the black suit he had arrived in. I was certain it was the only one he possessed. His bangs of white hair were imprisoned by his black hat, except, of course, the thick fringe that lay on the back of his neck. The Booher farm had never seen a stranger figure than Dr. Langsner.

Despite the heat of the day and his unsuitable clothes, he appeared quite cool and composed, and we followed him as he walked slowly to the back of the house. He reminded me of the old water-diviners who used a hazel twig to discover a hidden well, except that he had nothing in his hand.

For twenty minutes or so he quartered the ground and then, apparently, got the scent and hurried ahead. We followed, and he stopped somewhere between the bunkhouse and one of the linden trees. His eyes were closed and he drew his hand over his brow.

"*Ja, ja! Ach Gott!*" he exclaimed. "I have it now. If you will take about ten big steps forward."

Leslie was the nearest to him and began to count the steps. At the ninth he stumbled and bent down. We hurried over, and there was the rifle lying in the grass.

"Oh no," said Inspector Longacre as if he could not believe what he saw. It was the murder weapon right enough, and it was lifted and wrapped very carefully. When we got back to Edmonton it would be examined for fingerprints.

"You will not find any," warned Dr. Langsner. "Vernon wiped the rifle very carefully and kept thinking of what he had done."

And so it turned out. In the meantime, though, I booked Vernon, not on suspicion of murder, but as a material witness, and he was placed in the jail at Edmonton "for his own protection."

"Would it be impertinent for me to tell you what I think should now be done?" asked Dr. Langsner.

We were only too willing to hear his opinion. It certainly appeared as if Vernon was the murderer, but we had to prove it, and at the moment we had not the semblance of a case against him. It would need much more conclusive evidence than Dr. Langsner's ability to read thoughts to convince any jury.

The little doctor then outlined his plan, and to meet his wishes we placed a chair outside Vernon's cell and saw to it that there was no unnecessary noise or interruption.

Dr. Langsner seated himself and then leaned forward to stare at Vernon through the bars. At first the young man appeared quite pleasant and tried to make conversation, but later he became angry and turned his back on the doctor. Dr. Langsner just sat there and stared. He was there for about an hour and then got up and said "Goodbye" to Vernon, but got no reply.

We were waiting for him in my office, and he said: "Vernon is guilty, there is not a shadow of a doubt about it. He killed his mother because he had come to hate her. I don't know the reason, but he has no regret. He walked into the kitchen to kill her, and she spoke to him without turning round. In his fury he fired three shots, and Fred, his brother, heard them. Vernon knew he had to kill him, although he did not want to, and he is sorry for it.

"When he ran out to hide the gun, he saw Rosyk and Cromby in the fields; he was sure Rosyk had seen him, and he killed him when he had the chance. Two hours later he decided that it was unsafe to allow Cromby to live. He felt he had to eliminate every possible witness."

I told the doctor that I thought his reconstruction of the murders was correct. "How can we prove it?" I asked.

"Find the woman," he said quickly, and when he saw he had us puzzled he explained:

"I do not know her name. Vernon stole the gun on the Sunday that Stevenson missed his weapon. He sneaked out of church, took it away and then returned. The woman who saw him leave was wearing a poke-bonnet. She has small eyes and a long jaw and she was sitting at the back of the church, to the left of the aisle. She saw him leave and watched to see if he would return."

"Find her," I said to Leslie, and he got up and went out immediately.

At noon the following day Leslie brought Erma Higgins to police headquarters. She was exactly as Langsner had described her and looked like an ancient pixie. She was a spinster and very much alert to what was going on around her, especially the flirtations between young people. Yes, she had seen Vernon leave and return later.

Now was the time to put the pressure on Vernon, but before he was brought into my room we set up the "scene." I sat at my desk and I had Erma Higgins and Dr. Langsner placed in the centre of the room facing the door, on either side of which stood Detective Leslie and Inspector Longacre. A chair was so placed that Vernon would face Miss Higgins and the doctor.

As soon as Vernon came in and sat down Miss Higgins said to him as she had been instructed: "Vernon, I saw you leave the church the day Charlie's rifle was stolen."

Vernon looked at her and then stared at the doctor.

"I know you did," he said heavily, "I know you did."

I heard the clock on the wall tick away the lost seconds and began to watch the gentle swing of the brass pendulum. Then Vernon turned a desperate face towards me and said pleadingly: "Let me confess. I killed them. Let me confess to you."

He began to sob, and his story was a broken account of a quartet of killings that had happened in the way Langsner had said. The motive was his rage against his mother. She was a woman of good deeds, but she ruled the home and she ruled Vernon, who was her favourite son. He had brought a girl to the house, the daughter of a farm worker, one Sunday whom Mrs. Booher had ordered out. Vernon believed he loved the girl and not only did his mother ridicule the attachment but she wounded him even more cruelly by telling him what she thought of his choice. He began to hate his mother, and when his talk of an elopement made no impression on her his resentment became murderous.

On April 26th, 1929, Vernon Booher was hanged for his fourfold murders.

Some months before, however, Detective Leslie and I drove Dr. Langsner to the station. He was leaving Edmonton and going north to Eskimo territory. I think he realised how grateful we were to him, even though we expressed our thanks so clumsily. Against his wishes he had accepted a small cheque, which, as I told him, was only a token tribute to his invaluable help.

As he left us he said with a rueful smile: "It is fine to make friends, but rather sad to leave them."

We shook hands and that was the last we saw of him. Time went by and then one day Detective Leslie laid a news clipping on my desk. It read:

"Maximilian Langsner, Ph.D. (University of Calcutta), was found dead yesterday in a small hut on the outskirts of Fairbanks, Alaska. Dr. Langsner was known for his theory on 'brain waves' and for his ability, often demonstrated, in reading the thoughts of other people. He was engaged in research on this subject at the time of his death.

"Dr. Langsner was widely known, and his undoubted gifts had been made use of by Royalty. He had solved mysteries for the Shah of Persia, the King of Egypt and had helped the British

Government in Asia. He will be remembered, too, for the assistance he gave to many police departments faced with difficult cases."

When I looked up from reading the news clipping Detective Leslie had left the room.

An Axe for Frau Marek

by Ex-Police Commissar Ignatz Peters, Vienna, Austria

L UCK, I am convinced, often can be misfortune in disguise, and if this were not true I should not now be telling you the story of Martha Löwenstein. She, of all people, had good reason to curse the day she thought she was lucky.

Many will remember her as a very beautiful girl, always stylishly dressed. Every day she took the electric car for Kirtnerstrasse, where she worked in a dress shop, from Ottakring, one of the shabbiest places in Vienna. It was a district of down-at-heel houses and depressed people, and Martha was one of the rare flowers that grew there. Men would put down their newspapers as soon as they saw her and always she had a bright smile for her fellow passengers.

She was well worth looking at, blonde, slim and with a fine complexion that certainly did not come from a box. Every day she wore something different and her elegance piqued the women to whom she was known by sight. They whispered that no girl from a poor neighbourhood could dress so expensively unless . . . well, that was what they said, but it was untrue. Martha was virtuous, and there was a simple explanation for everything.

She confided the truth to Moritz Fritsch, the owner of a large department store in Vienna and a wealthy and cultured man. He was in his sixties, but looked very much younger. He found an opportunity to speak to Martha one evening as she was on her way home. He told her that he had often seen and admired her and he complimented her on the way she dressed. Martha said she came from a very poor home and worked in a dress shop. Her employer had always been exceedingly kind, and treated her almost as a daughter.

"She likes to see me in good clothes," Martha said, "and says I am a splendid advertisement for her shop. But for her I should look as poor as do many girls who have to work for a living."

Herr Fritsch promptly offered to find her a well-paid job in his store, but the young girl would not hear of it. She was devoted to her employer and on no account would she leave her.

"I must say I admire your loyalty," said Fritsch. "But you will, of course, allow me to take you home?"

Martha stepped into the chauffeur-driven limousine, and on the way to Ottakring explained that she and her mother lived alone. Her father had emigrated to America many years before and they had not heard of him since.

Back at his villa at Mödling that evening, Moritz Fritsch could not get the girl out of his mind. Her home was deplorable, and so, too, was her mother, a hulk of a woman, vulgar and tactless. She had told him all there was to know about the family, and it had turned out that Martha was, in fact, a love-child and her daughter by adoption only.

Fritsch was divorced and his two children were married. Except for his servants he lived alone, and that night he felt how empty his home had become. He was very rich and very lonely.

Shortly afterwards he took Martha out to dinner, and not only showed her a glimpse of luxury but suggested that she should become his ward. It would give her, he said, the right to everything her beauty deserved—clothes and jewels, education and travel and the company of intelligent people.

Martha did not need to be persuaded, and the fashionable villa in the suburbs became her home. Fritsch kept his word. He sent her to a school for young ladies and, for holidays, to France and England. At eighteen Martha was more lovely than ever and she had acquired poise and social polish.

When she returned to live at the villa her benefactor introduced her to his friends at parties and dinners. He never refused her anything and soon she possessed more jewels and clothes than she could ever have dreamed of. However, when the gilt had worn off a little Martha began to suffer from the moods that harry all unfulfilled young women. Whenever she was in a tantrum Fritsch would buy her some new piece of jewellery and he seems to have understood just why his fascinating ward behaved as she did.

Fritsch's devotion to the girl had, of course, long been the subject of gossip, particularly among the servants. A maid said she had seen him embracing his ward in the garden and in a manner that was hardly fatherly. On another occasion they were together in Martha's bedroom, both rather carefree and lively from the champagne they had drunk.

Three years went by, and towards the end began a period during which Martha could not be roused from her black moods, despite all the presents Fritsch gave her. The old man felt, as he told his friends, that he was, perhaps, demanding too much from her and was certain that she feared the day when he would no longer be alive to protect her.

Fritsch was probably right, for when he told Martha that he had made a new will in which she had not been forgotten, she cried a little and put her arms round the old man. It was the end of her unhappiness. Fritsch by law was bound to leave a third of his estate to his ex-wife and he had settled money, too, on his children. Martha was to have what was left, including the house.

A year after this arrangement was made Fritsch died at the age of seventy-four. Present at the bedside were Martha, the old man's family and Dr. Pollack, his physician.

When the will was read Betty Fritsch was furious. "I do not understand it," she protested. "At the time of our divorce Moritz solemnly promised that the estate would be left to the family."

"I drew up the will according to Herr Fritsch's wishes," said the lawyer sharply.

But Betty was not to be persuaded. "My husband was old, but his health was good. I think this girl knows something about his death. There is only one way to find out. The body must be exhumed."

Everybody was horrified by the suggestion, particularly Fritsch's son and daughter. "Mother was always terribly jealous of Father's ward," said young Fritsch. "Under no circumstances must Father's body be disturbed."

There was no inquiry and Martha received her inheritance in due course, but got far less money than she had anticipated. Although she was not seen about much a handsome young man began to visit her at the villa, and three months after Fritsch's death it became known that she had married him. His name was Emil Marek and he was studying engineering. Martha had been meeting him secretly for over a year.

It was not until some time afterwards that I heard the name of Martha Löwenstein Marek for the first time, and it happened in this way. One day I got a telephone call from Herr Möller, the vice-president of an insurance company. He said he was at the Billroth Hospital and asked me if I would go at once to meet him there. Möller was waiting for me and we went into one of the smaller rooms of the hospital, where a man's leg, severed just below the knee, lay on a table. The shoe and sock had not even been removed.

Möller explained why he had called me at the *Polizei Dezernat*.

"The leg belongs, or rather belonged, to a young man named Emil Marek. He lives in a villa in the suburbs with his wife, and the maid telephoned me to say that he had injured himself badly while cutting down a tree in the garden. He was brought here and the surgeon who completed the amputation tells me the leg was hanging only by a sinew."

"Why were you telephoned about the accident, Herr Möller?"

"Because Marek is insured with us for a considerable sum of money."

Möller gave me the details. About a week before Marek had called on him to take out a policy by which he would be covered for £10,000 in the event of any serious accident. Marek told him he was studying engineering at the Vienna Technical Institute and not long ago had married a young woman who had money. The Government was interested in an electrification scheme for Burgenland which he had prepared, and he felt that it was only fair to his wife that he should be adequately insured against the possibility of an accident. He did not want to become a burden to her.

"I was dubious about the proposal," said Möller, "and refused to entertain it. All the same I was impressed by Marek. He seemed a very decent young man, honest and very intelligent. Later I wondered if I had done the right thing and made some inquiries. I found that he has a good name at the institute and I was able to confirm that he had told me the truth about the scheme he has put up to the Government. In fact, I became convinced that he was a good risk and made arrangements to issue the policy. He came back, signed the papers, and paid the premium."

We were still talking when Dr. Rudolf Küster came into the room, and Möller introduced him to me. "Marek has had a very narrow squeak," said the surgeon, "and if his wife had not used several tourniquets he would have bled to death before anything could have been done for him. He is very shocked and has lost a lot of blood, but he is young and healthy and should get over it."

I asked the surgeon the angle of the wound and he looked at me curiously.

"It is rather puzzling," he said. "The cut is almost straight, and it is difficult to say exactly how it happened, but an accident can often show a freakish result."

"If it was an accident," said Möller.

It was asking a lot to believe that a person would hack off his leg to collect insurance, but then one can never tell. Marek was far too ill to be questioned, but Martha, too, was detained at the hospital, for she had collapsed as soon as her husband had been taken into the operating theatre.

She had been given a sedative, but was conscious and able to talk. She cried as she told us that her husband had been cutting down a tree when the axe slipped. She had heard his cries and so had the neighbours. They had found him in a great pool of blood, and everybody had helped with the tourniquets while awaiting the ambulance which had been telephoned for.

Despite her pallor and distress she looked very elfin and lovely as she lay in the hospital bed. She murmured that she would always love her husband, and soon she was sleeping like a tired child.

In the meantime I sent Detective Carl Huber to the villa to have a look around, and he came back with some surprising news. In the garden was a half-felled tree, a great patch of blood and a razor-sharp axe. "Somebody had wiped the axe clean," said Huber. "There was not a spot of blood on it, nor a fingerprint."

It was possible of course that the axe had been wiped innocently by a maid or someone, but it was not possible to explain away the expert evidence Möller and I heard the following morning at the Vienna Medical Institute, to which the leg had been sent for examination.

Removing his pince-nez, which he wore attached to a silk cord,

Professor Meixner pointed to Exhibit A and said: "Gentlemen, there can be no question but that these wounds were inflicted deliberately. The partial amputation required three separate strokes of the axe, and the marks on the limb are plainly discernible, each going deeper than the previous one."

Quite involuntarily I exclaimed, "But that is incredible!" and then remembered that it is the incredible that gives the police their employment.

"What is credible," remarked Möller sagely, "is that Marek had help in mutilating himself."

"You mean his wife, I suppose?"

"Yes; I believe she can tell us what really happened."

There were many inquiries to be made before the Mareks could be arrested on a charge of attempted fraud, and, in any case, Emil Marek could not be moved from hospital for some time. I learned a lot about Martha and how she had become an old man's darling. The case was so unusual that it became the talk of Vienna, and Martha herself was astute enough to take part in the controversy.

Shortly after being released on bail she invited me to call on her at the villa. A smart little maid opened the door and showed me into the drawing-room, where I found her lying—Recamier-like—on a chaise-longue surrounded by an audience. The room, beautifully furnished, and with many rare pieces, was full of reporters, and Martha offered me her hand to kiss as if I were a courtier instead of a police officer.

"You must pardon me for not rising, but I am still very weak. I have invited the reporters here in order to tell them that my husband and I are being prosecuted at the instigation of an insurance company which hopes to evade paying the money it owes us."

She paused and gave me a cool stare, and I could see that she had won the sympathy of everybody present. "You see," she went on, "I have received certain information of which I am sure the police cannot be aware. It was given to me by a person who works at the hospital and he tells me that he had seen Herr Möller talking very confidentially with one of the surgeons. Later, and I am assured of the truth of this, this witness saw this selfsame surgeon extending the area of the wound on poor Emil's amputated leg."

This was sensational "copy" for the newspapers, and one of the reporters asked: "Can you tell us the name and occupation of your witness?"

Martha smiled a little sadly. "No, I am not able to say who he is, for reasons I am sure you will understand. He was kind enough to volunteer this information, and that is all I can tell you for the time being."

I stayed behind, and it took me a long time to secure from Martha the name of the person who was supposed to have witnessed an act of collusion between Möller and a surgeon. It was a very ugly allegation and not for one moment did I think it was true.

The person in question was a hospital orderly named Karl Mraz. He was a frail creature and not very intelligent. He bore out Martha's story when first questioned, but he did not stand up to the interrogation and finally admitted that Frau Marek had offered him 10,000 schillings if he would repeat the story she had concocted.

A further charge of attempting to obstruct the course of justice was added to the indictment when the two prisoners were tried, but they were not seriously inconvenienced.

Crime has an ugly face and nobody looked less like criminals than Emil Marek, a most handsome cripple, and Martha, his enchanting wife. They had the newspapers on their side too, and the charge of attempted fraud was dismissed for lack of sufficient evidence. On the second count they were found guilty and sentenced to four months' imprisonment, but it was ruled that since they had already spent a similar period in custody while awaiting trial the sentence had already been served.

Over coffee with Möller I could see he was very worried at the prospect of his company having to meet the Mareks' claim. Had I not been convinced that it was fraudulent I would not have offered him certain advice. I knew the history of Martha, and of the doubt in Betty Fritsch's mind that her husband had died a natural death, and advised him that Martha, quite literally, might not care to have her past dug up. I offered him this advice as a friend, and not as a police officer, and said that no doubt a little heart-to-heart talk with her might persuade her to accept a more modest settlement.

Möller dropped in at a party the Mareks gave to celebrate their freedom and he said enough to convince Martha that in the circumstances it would be wiser to settle for £3,000, which she did. After all the costs of the defence had been met Emil's amputated leg did not return much of a profit.

They had been very lucky to escape a long term of imprisonment, and it was because I felt so certain of their guilt that I kept an eye on them. The scandal of the trial ruined all prospects of Emil's electrification project, for the Government promptly withdrew its support and he could find nobody as a private backer. He tried to make money with a fleet of taxis he bought, but the venture was a costly failure and ended in the villa having to be mortgaged to meet his debts.

The Mareks disappeared for some time, and one of my detectives discovered they had gone to Algiers to manufacture radio sets for foreign markets. Labour was cheaper there and no doubt the couple regarded this move as a fresh start.

The next time I saw Martha I could hardly believe it was her. She was selling vegetables from a barrow on a street in one of the poorest sections of Vienna. She had not lost her looks entirely, but her face was drawn and angry. I stopped my car to speak to her.

"Yes," she said bitterly, "we're as poor as I look. Nothing has gone right for us. Emil's business failed in Algiers, and that meant the end of the villa, which was already mortgaged. This is what I have been reduced to. I escaped once from the filth and ugliness of poverty, but now I am a prisoner again."

Martha was wearing a soiled cotton dress and shoes that appeared too big for her. Her appearance would have horrified Moritz Fritsch. I realised how much she disliked me, but at least I was someone she could talk to. "We are really up against it. I have to do this to keep a bit of bread in our mouths. My husband is no longer able to work and we have a young daughter and a baby boy."

The Mareks had been knocked about pretty badly, but Martha was so viperish that it was difficult to feel any sympathy for her. I did not see her again for some time, but in July 1932 I read of Emil Marek's death in one of the newspapers. I got thinking about it and made some inquiries among neighbours. Emil, they said, had been ill for some time. There seemed to have been some paralysis, loss of vision and other painful symptoms. Martha, I was told, nursed him and did everything that was possible until neighbours made a collection among themselves and paid for an opinion by a specialist. Emil's illness was diagnosed as advanced tuberculosis and he was admitted to the charity ward of the Calvary Hospital, where he died soon afterwards.

These facts I was able to confirm, but I might not have been so convinced that Marek's death arose from natural causes had I known that a little over a month afterwards the death also occurred of his daughter, Ingeborg. In the rush of police work the event escaped my notice.

It was 1933 and Hitler already was in power and Europe's long night had begun. Five years of darkness and change went by, and in March 1938 the Nazis marched into my country, and nobody, not even those who welcomed the *anschluss,* could foretell what awaited them tomorrow. The past seemed completely wiped out and with it the record of one's own life and work. Perhaps that explains my feeling of astonishment when I again heard the name of Frau Marek.

She had, according to a report placed on my desk, been the victim of the theft of a number of valuable tapestries and paintings. She was living in Kuppelweisergasse, one of the better parts of the city, which was certainly an improvement on selling carrots, onions and potatoes to the underprivileged, as she had been doing when last I saw her.

I thought it would be interesting to call on her, and, at first, Martha did not recognise me. With a graceful gesture she indicated the bare walls of her large and handsome apartment. "They were stolen during the night," she said tersely. She looked at me a second time and with recognition. "Well, *how* very nice to see you again," she said, as if she actually meant it.

"You've had a change of luck," I said.

"Yes, indeed. This house was left to me by Mrs. Löwenstein, a relative of my father. Please do your best to recover the stolen articles."

Martha had plenty of nerve, I had to admit to myself. I said to her: "I suppose you had the valuables insured?"

"Naturally. Herr Neumann, who incidentally is a tenant here, issued the policy."

It was my turn to be surprised, and I wondered if she had been up to her old tricks again. Surely, I thought, she must have learned her lesson, but frauds invariably repeat their offences, and I decided it would be worth my while to make a few calls. If the robbery had been faked, then Frau Marek must have had the tapestries and

paintings removed, and eventually I found the removal firm who
had done the job. Martha had arranged for the collection to be made
at night-time and her valuables were in safe storage at the Omega
repository in Ottakring.

For the second time I arrested Martha on a charge of attempted
fraud. The newspapers had not forgotten her trial eleven years before, and, since she began once more to dominate the front pages,
things began to happen. While the fraud case against her was pending
a young man named Herbert Kittenberger called on me and told me
he was convinced that Frau Marek had poisoned his mother. He
wanted her body exhumed.

From what he told me, his mother, Felicitas Kittenberger, had
rented a room in Martha's apartment house and had died there after
a brief illness. Her son had not been told of her death until after the
funeral.

"Why not?" I asked.

Herbert Kittenberger said he had not even known of his mother's
illness. He admitted that he was often away looking for work, but
asserted that Frau Marek could have got in touch with him had she
wanted to. "I tried to get an explanation from her and she said she
had tried to find me, but I am certain she was lying."

Although Frau Kittenberger's doctor maintained that his patient
had died from natural causes I thought it advisable to apply for an
order to exhume her body. During the last few years death, it
seemed, had followed Martha around, and I sensed there was much
to be explained. It meant a lot of work and a lot of back-tracking,
but I found out that shortly after the death of her husband Martha
had moved into the home in Kuppelweisergasse of her aged relative,
Frau Susanne Löwenstein. In the neighbourhood there were still
those who remembered the old woman's pretty companion. Martha
had visited Frau Löwenstein to begin with, and had then persuaded
her that she needed someone to look after her.

Once again Martha was able to escape from poverty. She was still
young, just over thirty, and the old woman must have bought her
some clothes, for she dressed well and had apparently saved a few
of the jewels that Fritsch had bought her years before.

She did the cooking for Frau Löwenstein, read to her, and, according to a witness, when the old woman told her she intended leav-

ing her all she possessed Martha had replied: "Everything I do for you is a labour of love. I do not do it for money."

Frau Löwenstein did not long survive, and in her final illness the symptoms were similar to those reported of Martha's late husband—numbness in her legs, dim vision and a difficulty in swallowing. When she died she left Martha the house and a substantial parcel of money.

One of the persons I talked to about Martha was Herr Neumann, her insurance agent, and the occupant of a couple of rooms at her house. He was garrulous but co-operative.

"I first met Frau Marek in 1935," he said. "One could not but be impressed by her—she was very good-looking and had superb manners. We saw a great deal of each other and she used to confide in me. She had been extravagant and had run through the money Frau Löwenstein had left her. The house in Kuppelweisergasse was expensive to keep up and she asked my advice.

"I suggested that she rent me a couple of rooms to help her out, and later Frau Kittenberger joined our little family. Frau Marek became very fond of her."

"Really?"

"Oh, yes. They were the best of friends. You can't believe a word that Herbert, Frau Kittenberger's son, says. He was a great trouble to her. I can assure you of that. He could not keep a job and money ran through his hands.

"Frau Kittenberger told Martha that the little money she had would go in no time if Herbert got hold of it, and there would certainly not be enough left to bury her. Martha consulted me about the problem and I worked out an insurance policy for Frau Kittenberger. The money was to go to Martha, and it was just as well the arrangement was made, for she was decently buried when her time came."

"What was the amount of the policy?" I inquired.

"It was very little, about three hundred pounds."

It appeared logical to assume that if Martha had indeed murdered Frau Kittenberger it was not the first occasion she had killed, and it became necessary therefore to open the graves of Emil Marek, Ingeborg, her daughter, and Frau Löwenstein.

While awaiting the medical findings of each of the four autopsies a question that had irked my subconscious mind for some time was

suddenly liberated. What had happened to the other Marek child—
the little boy? On their return from Algiers Marek and his wife had
lived in Hitzing, and it was in this district of Vienna that detectives
traced the child, Alfons, who was boarded out with neighbours. He
was reported to be very ill.

The woman who looked after him told me that she feared little
Alfons was suffering from tuberculosis, which she believed he had
contracted from his father. The symptoms were greatly similar. Frau
Marek, she said, was a constant visitor and often arrived in time to
give him his evening meal. Frequently she brought him something
special to eat.

"Frau Marek is a very brave woman," said my informant with
tears in her eyes. "I heard her telling the little boy he would soon be
with his father, and she herself looked just like an angel."

"Don't you ever read the papers?" I asked her.

"Nein, Herr Peters. We are very poor."

We got the little boy into hospital, and during the trial of his
mother doctors had to fight hard to save his life.

Martha was charged with the multiple murders of her husband
and daughter and of those of Frau Löwenstein and Frau Kittenberger. All of them had died from one of the poisonous compounds
of thallium, and a pharmacist in Florisdorf produced records of sale
of the poison to Martha on a date prior to the death of each vicitm.
There was other evidence that dovetailed and proved the guilt of
the accused beyond all possible doubt.

White and tense, Martha heard the public prosecutor brand her
as a creature more vile than Lucrezia Borgia herself. With the advent
of Hitlerism the death penalty had been restored in Austria and
Martha was sentenced to be beheaded.

On December 6th, 1938, she was taken from her cell to the execution block. Her hands tied behind her, she knelt down to receive
the death-blow and her head was severed from her body in a single
and fearful swing of the axe.

I am not able to say what were her thoughts during the short time
she awaited the carrying out of the sentence. She may, of course,
as she had every reason to, have thought of the days when her beauty
attracted Moritz Fritsch and how lucky she had imagined herself
to be for the golden chance of turning her back on poverty. Ultimately, though, it had brought her face to face with murder.

Perhaps even as a young girl she had possessed the instincts of a killer, but it is just possible that had she remained poor she might well have stayed alive.

Who can say?

Blonde in the Jute Sack

by Superintendent Jeffrey Reid, Port-of-Spain, Trinidad, West Indies

A HOLLYWOOD PRODUCER is reported to have said to a lagging script-writer: "Never mind the dialogue, just tell me what the characters *say*." I believe I understand what he wanted—as little improvisation as possible, a blanket on half-formed intuitions and just the facts, the barer the better.

It is the kind of dictum that should undoubtedly apply to this, my strangest story, except that it happened in Trinidad, one of the tropical islands of the West Indies, where, despite the jingles of the calypso singers, facts do not always easily fit the situation, or even vice versa.

There are, I believe, about half a million people in Trinidad, the West Indians themselves, Hindus, lean Negroes from the African coast, Chinese, European immigrants, the British and the tourists; and just as many religions, beliefs, customs, social layers and taboos, and if you cannot understand that this can lead to a lot of complications then you must have been sitting too long in the sun!

The murder I intend getting around to, as soon as I can, was as much a product of Trinidad as the sugar-canes, and the fact that it took a long time to discover the author of it can be ascribed not to any lack of police enterprise but to those very intangibles I have already mentioned.

One day in April 1954, as I sat at my desk at headquarters at Port-of-Spain I was told that a fisherman had found on the shores of a quiet cove that the local inhabitants call Godinot Bay the body of an unknown woman wrapped in a jute sack, which had been packed with sand to prevent it floating.

Godinot Bay is about thirty-five miles south of Port-of-Spain, but there were still a few barefoot villagers standing near the body when my aide, Lieutenant Clark, and I arrived on the sunlit beach.

The body, I could see, would need more than a cursory glance to establish identification. It was that of a white woman and, from the appearance of the limbs, she had been quite young. More than that I was unable to tell, except that I recognised murder when I saw it.

We took the body to the hospital mortuary at San Fernando, the nearest town, for a post-mortem by the district medical officer, Dr. Russell W. Barrow. He was the son of a wealthy planter, good-looking and now married.

I knew the family by reputation. When Russell Barrow left the island to undertake two years' advanced study at King's College Hospital in London he was given a farewell party that was attended by the most prominent among the smart set. He was joined in London by Lucy, his attractive and vivacious sister, but her visit was cut short, and the story got around that she had returned home in consequence of a romance that had ended unhappily.

While we waited in San Fernando to hear the result of the preliminary examination I asked my colleague if he had any ideas about the dead woman.

"No," he said shortly. "It's a bit strange that nobody has been reported missing; at least, no white woman."

Dr. Barrow came in at last, looking warm and worried.

"I think she was strangled," he said, "but I'll know more when I complete the post-mortem. She's been in the water for several days, and this will surprise you, as it did me—she was literally eviscerated."

"Looks pretty grim."

"Yes. A six-inch incision was made to clear out the intestinal tract. Grim is the right word. It will take a little time, but I'll give you a full report as quickly as possible."

Before I could get over my surprise Lieutenant Clark asked Dr. Barrow if the technique of evisceration was difficult.

"Not to anyone with medical knowledge," he said, "or even to those who are accustomed to killing animals. Why it was done I can't say."

News travels as fast on our island as it does in any village, and everybody seemed to know that a white woman had been murdered, and strange things done to her before she was tied in a jute sack and thrown into the sea.

Dr. Barrow arrived that afternoon, much earlier than I had anticipated. He told me the victim was a blonde, between twenty-five and thirty years of age, and that the cause of death was strangulation. The jugular vein had been cut to bleed the body after death and it had been done before the act of evisceration. Barrow laid on my desk a gold filling from one of the teeth of the victim and a charm bracelet and a medallion which were found among the sand in the jute sack.

As I was examining these finds Dr. Barrow said something had happened which had given him quite a jolt. I asked him to explain, and he said: "Well, while I was engaged on the autopsy Dr. Singh arrived. I suppose you know him?—he's from the city here."

I knew Dr. Singh well enough . . . Dr. Dalip Lutchmie Persad Singh, son of a Hindu couple who had settled in Trinidad in the twenties as indentured servants and had later become well to do as a result of shrewd investments. They had three children, of whom Dalip was the most troublesome. He had left the island to study medicine in Scotland and he was to have come back to marry a Hindu bride who had been chosen for him. Instead, he had returned with a German wife, and this had been a great shock to his parents.

Dr. Barrow said he had known Singh in England, but had seen very little of him in Trinidad, and I knew why. He was greatly surprised when Singh appeared during the autopsy.

"We looked at the body together," continued Dr. Barrow, "and I asked Singh if he happened to know who it was, and he said he did not. We talked for a little while and he borrowed a few of my textbooks and then left. I have a feeling, though, that Singh came to see what he expected to find. In other words, he knew whose body it was on the table."

I asked the doctor to tell me how well he knew Singh in England, and Barrow flushed.

"We saw quite a lot of him—if that's what you mean, Superintendent. You know how it is when people from the same place meet in another part of the world. Of course, here it is different, we don't move in the same circles."

"That isn't quite what I meant. How did you get to know him in the first instance? You were in London and he was in Edinburgh."

Dr. Barrow looked very uncomfortable, but he was frank. "It was through my sister Lucy. She came to England on the invitation of my wife and me, and, on the way out, met Dalip Singh. It was one of those shipboard romances and Lucy took it seriously. We were dismayed, very dismayed. I don't think Lucy would have looked twice at Dalip Singh had she met him here, but there it was, and my wife and I tried to do our best in the circumstances. It seemed as if she would marry him until he met Inge."

She was the woman Dr. Singh had married and brought back to Trinidad. She was very Nordic, very intelligent and very witty. Those who met her socially liked her and she was quite expert at mixing new cocktails and a strange drink she called Ananas-Bowle, which was a concoction of champagne, white wine, rum and pineapple. She was, too, a qualified optician and not only established herself professionally in Port-of-Spain but visited the neighbouring islands of St. Vincent, Grenada and St. Lucia.

"Did you know Inge when you were in London?" I asked Barrow.

"Yes, Singh had the audacity to bring her to the house, introduce her to Lucy, and then announce his engagement to her to the three of us."

I was now aware of how Barrow felt about Singh. The young doctor had not been anxious to be reminded of the past, but I had wanted answers to the questions I had asked him and that was all there was to it.

Now, as a result of what he had told me, it was necessary to have a talk with Dr. Singh himself, and he returned with Lieutenant Clark not long after Barrow had gone. Dr. Dalip Singh was short, but his tailor knew how to offset his lack of inches. He was impeccably dressed and, despite the heat, looked exceedingly cool. As usual, he wore a pair of dark glasses.

"Thank you very much for coming, Dr. Singh," I said. "We have the unidentified body of a woman in the hospital morgue at San Fernando. This medallion and charm bracelet belong to her. Can you identify them?"

I did not expect Singh to wilt in the way he did. He seemed to fold up completely. "Yes," he said with a wild look at the sad little relics, "they belong to my wife, Inge."

"Do you know where she is?"

"I don't. I only wish I could tell you."

"When was the last occasion that you saw her?"

"It was on the night of April 6th."

"I think you had better tell me about it."

"She just walked out. I didn't want to start any gossip, because I knew she would return. When I heard that a body had been found yesterday I went to the San Fernando hospital, but it did not appear to be that of my wife. I am sure it is all a mistake. She will come back, I know it!"

"Come now, Dr. Singh," I said with some irritation. "I want to know why your wife should walk out. You must know. Was there a quarrel over another man?"

"No, I assure you there was not. It is not unusual for her to go off like this. She has always been the victim of periodic depressions, and at such times she wanted to be alone. I know she has been away longer than usual and I had thought of calling you. But I am sure you will understand my reluctance."

I understood all right, although not as Dr. Singh would have me believe. I apologised for taking up his time and also for having to tell him that the woman in the jute sack was his wife . . . whether he believed it or not.

The investigation was a slow affair. Both Lieutenant Clark and I suffered from a sense of guilt, but we had to feel our way carefully and painstakingly. However, an interesting interview took place with the parents of Dr. Dalip Singh. The doctor's mother immediately expressed the keenest pleasure at the news that her daughter-in-law was on longer in the land of the living.

"She should be dead. She was no good!" she said in judgment.

"In what way was she 'no good'?" I asked.

"She smoked, drank and behaved as no woman should. She displayed her bosom and wore her skirts up to her knees. That is something a Hindu woman does not do. Modesty forbids it."

Dr. Singh's mother was the spokesman. Her husband just clasped his hands together and allowed her to talk. He did not say a word.

To find the Singhs' East Indian houseboy, a character named Kramchand Ramsahaye, Clark and I went out to the native quarter, where the yards were filled with chickens, pigs, and here and there a stray dog. Ramsahaye lived in an unpainted shack with a family named Boyeur. When we located the houseboy he was playing with half-naked children, but he himself was cleanly attired and obviously took great pride in his appearance.

When I asked him if he worked for Dr. Singh his answer was so emphatic that I knew it was the doctor he liked and not his wife.

"How is it you do not care for your mistress?"

"She is cruel and a barbarian. She never asks, she yells. She gets drunk, and no woman of respect gets drunk. She slap me and my friends here."

"Why are you here today instead of taking care of the house for Dr. Singh?"

Ramsahaye sighed. "Uncle Doc say he no longer need me. I must find another house to work in. Now that the mistress is dead I cannot go back."

"Do you remember the last day you saw her?"

"It was April 6th. Of that I am sure."

I asked the houseboy to bring his friends, the Boyeurs, to talk to us, and he padded off and brought back Enid Boyeur, a tall handsome West Indian, George, her husband, whose skin was lighter, and their son. Enid, dressed in a French skirt and with her hair knotted in a handkerchief, told me she sold fruit and vegetables to Dr. Singh and his wife.

"Did you like them?"

"Yes, I did."

"Ramsahaye says you didn't like her."

Enid glared at the houseboy. "But I did like her!"

"Did she ever strike you?"

Enid would not answer, and it was the same with her husband and son. George Boyeur looked after the garden at the Singh house and his son helped him. Both of them said they did not dislike the doctor's wife, but they would not answer when I asked if she had ill-treated them.

I could see the Boyeurs were displeased with Ramsahaye, but the houseboy had the last word in the muttering that went on between them. Quite suddenly he seized young Boyeur, pulled up his shirt and revealed a livid scar on his back. "You like her, huh?" he said in disgust.

One important discovery made by Lieutenant Clark, and on our own doorstep, was that ten days before Inge Singh was found on the beach she lodged a nuisance complaint that somebody had placed a circle of white chicken feathers on the steps leading to the veranda of her home. She appeared to think it was done just to annoy her, and did not realise, as we did, that she had enemies among the natives, enemies who wished to see her dead.

Lieutenant Clark had got out a file on natives who had been killed from revenge and said: "Some of the natives are not so far removed from the jungle that they have lost their belief in supernatural powers. This business of the chicken feathers may mean something."

"You think she was killed by native decree? It's a possibility, of course, particularly the way it was done and the evisceration."

The newspapers began to hint that the police were not too anxious to uncover a scandal involving people high in the social register, but Clark and I were not to be hurried into any false move. On May 7th a note mysteriously appeared on my desk. It was written in pencil, hardly intelligible, and read as follows:

I want to tell you that you are on the rong track. Mr. Don Bain was he come gave me £100 to help in the job. He give me only £30. That night Mr. Bain carry me to a house in Marli St., he a white man they call Doc with glass on he eye and the next man they call Ches bring the bag in a car P1020. I sorry for Dr. Singh he is not guilty. Mr. Ches take the bag in the boat to Godinot then put him in schooner. I today give back the Dr. Singh the passport and bracelet.

We didn't take up a lot of time discussing the note. It stank, but it gave us an idea to work on, and Clark took it away with him convinced that it could be made to fulfil a certain purpose.

Forty-eight hours later, at seven o'clock in the evening, I ordered the arrest of Dr. Singh for the murder of his wife. It was not until November 1st, 1954, however, that his trial began in the Supreme Court Chamber in Port-of-Spain's Hall of Justice before Mr. Justice Mortimer Duke.

Dr. Singh was as immaculately dressed as ever, and throughout the trial he conferred constantly with his brother, Indas, who is an attorney.

It took the Crown Prosecutor, Mr. Malcolm Butt, four hours to open the case, and he said it would be proved beyond all doubt that the accused murdered his wife out of jealousy.

The first witness called was Lloydie Johnson, a private detective, who said that Dr. Singh visited his office about three weeks before the death of his wife. He was terribly upset because he said his wife had committed adultery with Ches Gibbs, a native assistant administrator for St. Vincent.

"What was the purpose of Dr. Singh calling on you?"

"He offered me a large sum of money if I would confront his wife and tell her that I had shadowed her and Gibbs and knew what had taken place. I told Dr. Singh that I could not be involved in anything so dishonest."

This evidence by an independent witness established the motive for the crime, and other witnesses helped to build up the case against Dr. Singh so that the court was given a full account of his movements on April 6th. Dr. Singh on that day met his wife at Piarco airport, on her return from St. Vincent, and drove her to her bank where she withdrew about £650.

Clarita George, cook at the Singh house, said she had served the doctor and his wife with lunch that day. They went out together and returned for evening dinner about seven o'clock. She identified the dress found on the body as one she had pressed for her mistress on April 6th and which Inge had worn at both meals.

Kramchand Ramsahaye, the houseboy, said that on the same night he was in the garden when he overheard a fierce quarrel between the Singhs. "Uncle Doc said, 'I do not think I could make a living with you any longer,' and later I could hear him beating her."

Ramsahaye heard Singh take the car out of the garage about eight-fifteen that evening and also his return about two o'clock in the morning. Later he asked the houseboy to wash down his car, and in ordering breakfast for himself only said his wife had gone out early.

Mrs. Plimmer, of the Northern Optical Company, whose offices were on the same floor as the doctor's wife, testified that on April 7th she asked Singh where his wife was. "She is out of town," he replied.

She asked him again the following day and he said: "It is none of your business. Keep your nose out of our affairs. Since you want to pry let me tell you that she is no good and is having an affair with a man on St. Vincent. I can tell you I should have followed the advice of my parents and married the girl they wanted for me. I lost a big dowry and got a no-good when I married Inge."

Dr. Barrow's wife, Sylvia, gave evidence the following day. She said that on the morning the body was found she received two long-distance calls from Dr. Singh, who wanted to speak to her husband. Singh turned up several hours later, and she directed him to the hospital, where her husband was engaged on the autopsy.

Dr. Barrow himself said the cause of death was strangulation. He believed the removal of the viscera was done to prevent the body from floating. A copy of Hamilton Bailey's *Emergency Surgery* was produced, and Dr. Barrow said that if the slitting of the windpipe took place after death there would be little bleeding. The book gave a description of the operation for the removal of the viscera.

Gaston Anderson, counsel for Dr. Singh, in his cross-examination of Barrow suggested that his testimony was poisoned by his dislike of the accused for jilting his sister, Lucy Barrow. Counsel suggested that the operation described by the witness could not have been done in such a short time or without proper equipment and lighting.

Altogether the prosecution called forty-five witnesses, including a famous Trinidad surgeon, Dr. Richard Acton, who said the accused had borrowed the medical book from him some time around April 1st, and Lieutenant Clark, who testified that the anonymous letter received at police headquarters was, in fact, written by the accused himself.

The defence pounced on Clark as a witness with only an elementary knowledge of graphology, but he coolly pointed out that the letter was written on a certain type of paper which Dr. Singh had in his office and which was not sold in any of the island's stationery stores, of which there were twenty-eight.

As the trial drew to its close—it lasted twenty-six days—Singh lost his dapper appearance and had, in fact, grown a beard. He elected not to give evidence, and he was found guilty and sentenced to death.

The execution by hanging took place on the rainy, humid morning of June 28th, 1955, and thousands lined the streets leading to the Royal Gaol until the news filtered through that Singh had died on the rough scaffold in the prison yard. There was a crowd, too, waiting at Bourne's Road Cemetery as Singh's coffin was lowered into the ground to join the company of Trinidad's criminals and paupers.

Motive for Murder

by Oldrich Adamec, Criminal Division of the Central Office of Public Security, Prague, Czechoslovakia

THAT APRIL AFTERNOON, as the raindrops sparkled on the deep breast of the Vltava, the old watchman at one of the locks looked out on the river at Prague, not, as Smetana had once done, to write a poem in music to the fast-flowing and noble wanderer from the Bohemian Forest, but with a speculative eye, as if he anticipated trouble.

He was a crusty old man, this watchman, but he loved the river and hated to see it affronted by the rubbish abandoned by boatmen and also by those who walked its banks. As he had half expected, he soon saw something that displeased him, and, with a shake of his head that was a silent condemnation of his fellow citizens, he picked up a boat-hook and pulled in a hefty parcel that was far too big not to arouse his suspicions.

He did not like the look of it at all, and he liked it even less when he got it open. Underneath the outer covering was a blanket, which he pulled aside to disclose the quartered body of a woman. The amputated legs and arms had been tied together and then secured to the torso. The old man then waddled away muttering to himself. The things people got up to nowadays—it was unbelievable. Well, this was the business of the police and he would ring them up and tell them what he had just pulled out of the river.

An examination of the butchered victim provided us with a couple of clues that were of first-rate importance. There was a great scar on the trunk which was the result of an operation, a thoracoplasty, as we were to learn later. Secondly, the remains had been wrapped not in one but in a pair of blankets, on each of which adhered a number of dog hairs.

Our first task was to find out who the victim was. We checked our list of missing persons, found that she was not among them, and turned to the hospitals to see if it was possible to identify her through the operation she had undergone.

About three o'clock in the morning we got a call from one of the city hospitals to say that the description we had given them suggested that the victim was one of their former patients, Madame Maria Vlchek, who had undergone a thoracoplasty. She was a young married woman, and the earliest information we had about her was that her employers had been looking for her ever since she had failed to return from the bank, where she had been sent to collect a large sum of money for staff wages.

The victim's husband, Jan Vlchek, identified his wife by the operation scar. He told us that when he realised she had disappeared he began to search for her, but he was unable to trace her movements after she had left the bank. He knew her employers thought she had absconded with the money, but he could not believe she would steal. She was a woman of excellent character, as he had every reason to know.

"Was your wife fond of a car ride?" I asked Jan Vlchek.

"Yes, she was indeed. But she would never have got into the car of a stranger. Of that I am certain."

The more I thought about the murder the more convinced I became that the killer had possessed a car. He could not possibly have dumped the body in the Vltava without taking it there in a car in the first place. At the factory where she worked we were told that Madame Vlchek had left at about eleven-twenty-five on the morning of April 17th to pick up the payroll at the Czechoslovak National Bank, which was only a short distance away. She told one of her colleagues that she would return immediately but she was not seen again. She arrived at the bank on time and a clerk remembered paying out the money to her. She was alone. There was no question of her being abducted as she left the bank. It was a busy quarter and anything untoward would have been noticed.

The only likely explanation was that Madame Vlchek had met somebody outside the bank whom she knew and had been persuaded, perhaps on some pretext, to get into a car. The encounter may have been a chance affair, but it had led to murder.

All this was conjecture, of course, but, as we were to discover, it was not far from the truth, and, by following this line of reasoning, we were able to arrest Madame Vlchek's murderer twenty-four hours after we had proved her identity. We had not much to work on in our search for the culprit, and we began by checking on the friends and acquaintances of the dead woman, especially those who owned a car.

For various reasons we were able to reduce the list of suspects quite quickly, and finally we became interested in a thirty-three-year-old accountant, Karl Jelliner, who lived with his wife and two children just outside Prague, and who knew Madame Vlchek and her husband very well. He had owned a car up to a month ago, when he had sold it.

We asked Jelliner to give an account of his movements, and he did so, coolly and precisely. He said that he went to work every day by bus and tram and had followed this routine on April 17th, the day of Madame Vlchek's disappearance. He admitted that during the morning he had left his office, but said he had returned at one o'clock.

We found out otherwise. Jelliner returned to his office at least an hour later than he claimed, and, significantly, in a suit different from the one he had worn earlier that day. This change of clothes was noticed by his colleagues.

In a further interrogation, on this occasion at his office, Jelliner appeared far less sure of himself. He was unable to answer many of our questions and became hesitant and very confused. We intercepted a telephone call for him from a woman, discovered who she was, and began to ask him about his association with her. He admitted she was his mistress. The fact that he was not quite so respectable as he had pretended to be was not in itself damning—it is a common human failing—but he confessed that his paramour liked a gay life and that they often visited one or another of the city's night clubs. I wondered how he had managed to pay for this on his modest earnings.

It will be remembered that on the blankets wrapped round the mutilated body of Madame Vlchek we found a number of dog hairs, and I knew I had found the answer to this part of the problem when we visited the apartment of Jelliner's mistress during her absence. She owned a little fox terrier whose coat—as an analysis showed—matched the hairs on the blankets. Nor was this the only discovery. There were bloodstains on the floor of the living-room and in the bathroom, and they belonged to the victim's blood group.

Quite near to Jelliner's place of employment we found an abandoned car in which were more hairs belonging to the fox terrier. The car was owned by a waiter named Slansky, and he provided us with the final page missing from the murder story. Two days before the crime took place Jelliner borrowed the car for an indefinite period and paid Slansky a sizeable sum for the privilege of driving it away.

Jelliner showed no surprise when we arrested him along with his paramour. He knew much more about accountancy than he did of criminology. No doubt he had believed that the Vltava would not yield up its dead and that Madame Vlchek's disappearance would come to be accepted as a mystery in which an embezzler had got clean away. He now admitted his guilt, and did his utmost to protect his mistress, whose expensive appetites had driven him to commit an atrocious crime. He said he alone had planned the murder and that his mistress was not present when he killed Maria Vlchek.

Jelliner and his woman had lived dissolutely, and, at first, he had tried to raise money fraudulently. When his schemes failed he began to think of Madame Vlchek's visits to the bank every week. He knew she always came away with a large amount of money. He was leading a double life—he had a wife and children to care for and he was supporting a woman who wanted much more money than he could give her. The thought that he might lose her to a richer man became intolerable and he decided to murder Madame Vlchek.

On the morning of April 17th he asked his superior at the office for time off to attend to some personal business in another part of the city. He had planned it all very carefully, cleverly he thought, and was in time to watch Madame Vlchek enter the bank. He had parked his car a little way down the street, and when she came out they met, as if by accident. He knew about the typewriter she wanted to sell and he spoke easily and confidently.

"I'll pay whatever you want for it," he said. "I know it's a good machine and, really, it's just what I want. Look, I have a car here.

Let's go to my aunt's apartment and I'll pay you there. You can give me a receipt and I'll collect the machine from you this evening."

Madame Vlchek had demurred, not because she was in any way suspicious of Jelliner's intentions, but she wanted to get back as quickly as possible to the factory with the money.

Jelliner reassured her. "Don't worry about being late in getting back. The apartment is quite close, and, in any case, I'll drive you back to the factory."

The "aunt's" apartment was the one he shared with his mistress, and Maria Vlchek had been done to death as soon as she had entered it and the door had closed behind her. Jelliner's paramour swore that she was absent at the time and did not even know of her lover's plan to rob and murder. She confessed, though, that she had helped him when she got back to the apartment and found what had taken place. Jelliner had quartered the body by then, and there was a lot of blood to clean up and the clothes and trinkets of the dead woman to be got rid of. As soon as it was dark Jelliner had parcelled up the body and taken it away in his car to dump it in the Vltava.

The case came before the Prague judges not as a conspiracy between two persons, but simply as a case of murder against Jelliner alone. His confession was placed before the court, and, having been found guilty, he was executed shortly afterwards.

Brides under the Hearth

by Detective-Sergeant Considine, Ex-C.I.D., Victoria, Melbourne, Australia

THE LAST TENANT of the villa in Andrew Street, Melbourne, had moved out about eight weeks before, and on this occasion it was not Connor, the agent, who was showing a new prospect over the place, but Mr. Stamford, the owner.

Everything looked rosy for a rental until they came to one of the bedrooms, and there the stench was so bad that the prospect pulled out a handkerchief to protect himself from further assault, gave Mr. Stamford a look of reproach, and hurried out of the villa.

Mr. Stamford did not much care for the smell either, and gave his agent hell for allowing the property to get into a state that drove people out of it.

Connor, however, could not quite understand the situation. When he had let the villa to the last tenant it was then in good condition. He went round to have a look at the place, particularly at the bedroom about which Mr. Stamford had so forcibly complained. He found it pretty ripe, and he felt it unfair to himself to remain a second longer than was necessary, but he was a conscientious man and saw that the new concrete hearthstone had not been there when he was last in the bedroom.

Whoever had laid the concrete had not taken into account the fierce heat of an Australian summer and the cement had dried out much too quickly, so that the hearth had begun to crumble. Connor realised that it was the source of the overpowering smell and he began to kick away lumps of soft concrete. Soon he found himself staring at part of the decaying corpse of a young woman.

He got out of the villa at the double and brought back with him Sergeant O'Laughlin and a couple of other police officers. Sergeant O'Laughlin was just heaving aside the last of the broken hearthstone when I arrived with Detective Cawsey, my aide. The body was that of a woman of about thirty. She had been fiendishly battered and her throat cut from ear to ear.

I asked Connor who had been the last tenant and he replied: "A man named Drewen. He took the place on December 16th and paid three weeks' rent in advance. He seemed all right and I didn't ask for references. In any case, he told me he had just arrived from England and knew nobody in Australia."

"Was he married?"

"He said he had his wife with him and wanted a house quickly because his hotel expenses were too high."

Connor was vague concerning Drewen's appearance, but I got a fair description of him from the neighbour next door, and also an account of what had happened during his stay at the villa.

"He was a funny sort of chap," said the neighbour. "I saw him a few times and tried to be friendly with him, but he wasn't buying. A few days before his wife moved in—I suppose it was his wife—Drewen had a bag of cement and some tools delivered, and, from the noise I heard later, I guessed that he was very busy in the house.

"His wife arrived on Christmas Eve with several trunks covered with labels, and it looked as if she had not long disembarked. Shortly after they began to quarrel, and the row went on until midnight. I never heard her voice again, but early next morning I could hear Drewen banging and hammering. I didn't see him during the next couple of days; not until he went out and returned with a carrier, who took away some luggage. As for his wife, I never saw her again."

Drewen was apparently about five feet seven inches, fair moustache and beard, aged about forty, and mild-mannered. His accent was English. The description was passed on to half a dozen detectives, who began a search for him among the hotels in the city. Enquiries, too, were made at the offices of every shipping company, and among carriers to find who had moved his luggage.

In the meantime Cawsey and I returned to the villa and a search turned up a few things that were informative—the front page of a mining magazine, a charred medicine bottle, the label of which still retained the first three letters of the word "poison," and a few storm matches similar to those used on ships.

The indications were that Drewen was a mining engineer and we knew already that he had not been in Australia long. Cawsey was on his knees in front of the fireplace when, from among the rubbish, he fished out a small invitation card.

"Listen to this," he said excitedly, and began to read: " 'Mr. Albert Williams requests the pleasure of the company of . . . at dinner at the Commercial Hotel, Rainhill.' "

Neither of us had heard of Rainhill before, but we found it in a gazetteer. It was a small township in Lancashire, roughly between St. Helens and Liverpool.

Cawsey said: "Williams could be our man. The card is blank and he must have been the host for it to be in his possession. I think Drewen is also Williams."

We discovered very quickly that Drewen or Williams had a liking for aliases. As reports began to come in from our outside men we found that he had bought the cement and tools in the name of Dobson and had used another name in arranging for the carriage of his luggage.

The name of Dobson was not unfamiliar to me. Just before the New Year a man using this name, and whose description was similar to that we had of Drewen, had swindled Kilpatrick & Company, a Melbourne firm, of some valuable jewellery. He had also tried to pull off another *coup* which would have cost another firm, McLean Brothers & Rigg, £2,000 had it succeeded.

The newspapers were given the story of the swindle and it brought results from five people who were on the same ship on the journey from England. He was known to them as Albert Williams and one woman passenger said of him:

"It was easy to be taken in by him. He was well mannered and affable, but a trickster and very fond of women. Everybody on board knew of his affairs with different women, except his wife. When he arrived in Melbourne he tried to get money out of three of his fellow passengers by putting up mining schemes that were obviously bogus."

Another passenger on the trip said:

"Williams told me he was a mining engineer. Engineering happens to be my profession too, and I would say he had had some experience of practical mining and knew what he was talking about. He was good with hand tools and had made himself a pair of pliers out of a couple of knitting needles. The workmanship was excellent. He was very proud of these pliers and liked showing them to everybody."

It was an old story—this foible of the criminally minded. Such men might change their appearance and turn up in the most unexpected places, but they could not alter their habits and often unwittingly betrayed themselves.

When we had interviewed the last of Drewen's shipboard acquaintances Cawsey commented: "We'll need to work fast to catch up with him. He certainly does not let the grass grow under him."

Drewen worked to a close programme and moved around quickly. He had reached Melbourne on December 15th, rented the villa the next day and ordered the cement and tools on the 17th. He fixed up the murder trap during the two following days, and pulled a couple of swindles on the 20th and 22nd. On the 24th he killed his wife and, four days later, stole the jewellery. On January 2nd he tried to rob McLean's.

Before his disappearance he had found time to "work" on three of his fellow passengers. Later we got to know that he had used eight different aliases and had stayed at six different hotels within a fortnight. During this period he had made appointments with two women, introduced to him by a matrimonial agency, and had written to seven others saying that he wanted to get married immediately. Finally, he became engaged to a young girl.

We had cabled Scotland Yard for information a few hours after the murder at the villa had been discovered, and, when we received a lengthy reply, it became even clearer to us why Drewen or Williams was an indefatigable traveller.

Drewen, in the name of Williams, had married a Miss Emily Mather at Rainhill and had sailed to Australia with her the previous November. At the request of the Yard the Rainhill police had searched a house he had lived in prior to taking Miss Mather as his bride. When the hearthstone was removed the searchers found the bodies of a woman and four children. Drewen was neither Drewen nor Williams. His real name was Frederick Bailey Deeming, a mining engineer who had worked for some considerable time in the South African goldfields.

This news put us in an ugly spot. Deeming was now revealed as a practised killer and that endangered any girl or woman prepared to accept his attentions. We alerted every police department and station throughout the country, knowing from our far-flung inquiries that he had not left Australia.

I had to decide, however, whether it was advisable to get the newspapers to help find him or wait and see if the net we had spread for him would deliver him into our hands. If we used the newspapers there was sure to be someone who would recognise him wherever he was, but the advantage could be double-edged. It could also tip off Deeming that he was wanted, and there were many places in which he could hide—remote mining camps and even within the deep bush itself.

But above all else we had to prevent his next murder, and I did not know a better way of doing it than through the newspapers. The same day that we issued a description of the wanted man, we learned from the Johannesburg police that in three houses in which he had lived they had dug up bodies from under each hearth.

When the announcement of our search for him was published it began to produce results at once. We learned that Deeming had sailed from Melbourne for Sydney on January 12th on the coaster *Adelaide*. He had a new alias for this occasion and passed himself off as Baron Swanston. Travelling on the same ship was a Miss Kate Rounsefell, a pretty eighteen-year-old heiress, and by the end of the two days' trip, due to Deeming's power over the opposite sex, the girl believed him to be as madly in love with her as she imagined herself to be with him.

It had been arranged between them that Deeming would visit her home to ask her parents for formal permission to marry her, but he had a certain chore to perform when he disembarked at Sydney on January 14th—he had to find a firm which could be swindled, and in this he experienced no difficulty.

A little later he presented himself at the Rounsefell home, and, such was his personal charm and power of persuasion, that he got the girl's parents to agree to an announcement of their engagement being made immediately. It was arranged, too, that Deeming's bride-to-be would follow him within a fortnight to Western Australia,

where, ostensibly, the marriage was to take place. Having tied everything up to his satisfaction, Deeming sailed the next day from
Sydney for Fremantle on the *Oceana*.

He was already in Western Australia by the time we learned all
this, and we telegraphed the police at Perth asking them to pick up
Deeming, alias Baron Swanston, not on a charge of murder, but for
having swindled Kilpatrick's, the jewellers.

The Western Australian authorities responded promptly. They
traced Deeming to the mining town of Southern Cross, which is
300 miles from Perth, and found that he had rented a house already and thoughtfully ordered supplies of cement and sand, as
he had done when he was in Melbourne.

Miss Rounsefell was to be the next bride to be tucked under the
hearth, but Deeming never saw her again. He had committed in
Melbourne the last murder he was ever to perpetrate, and was
returned to that city. At his trial, before Mr. Justice Hodges, Deeming hardly glanced at the array of witnesses as, one after the other,
they gave evidence which progressively tightened the noose round
his neck.

He appeared quite unconcerned and took more interest in the
spectators than in what was said against him. He could hardly have
not realised that there was no escape for him. There were nine other
murders on the file, and no killer ever went into court more hope-
lessly enmeshed than Deeming. He was found guilty of murder
of Emily Mather, his bride from Rainhill, and was executed at
Melbourne Jail.

Case of the Headless Corpse

by Police Chief Antonio A. Afonso, Policia
Judiciaria, Lisbon, Portugal

THE DEAD, happily for them, are beyond insult, but I have read somewhere that no one is as friendless as those who lie unburied. I think this must have been in my mind when I heard about the headless corpse a shepherd had found beneath an ilex tree on grazing land eighteen miles from the town of Alcacer do Sal in the province of Alentejo.

I read of the murder in a newspaper on the morning of June 22nd, 1953, and it seemed to me not only a shameful way for a man to be killed, but quite terrible that his corpse, in some rude barn, had to wait for someone to come along and say: "Yes, I know this body from the neck downwards."

At the Policia Judiciaria in Lisbon we were not directly concerned with the murder, which was a matter for the local police. But I could not get the affair out of my head and wondered if anybody would remember to take the fingerprints of the dead man. It was a sure way of finding out who he was, since every Portuguese national is fingerprinted when issued with an identity card.

They will bury him without taking his prints, I thought, and it worried me so much that I talked to my superior, the sub-director of the Policia Judiciaria, about it and suggested we send a reminder to the local authorities. "It isn't that I distrust the country police," I said, "but they are not accustomed to dealing with murder."

"Afonso," he said, "you are quite right. We will send a telegram to the public prosecutor at Alcacer do Sal suggesting this should be done."

Six days later we received a request from this official for help in investigating the crime, and that was how it came about that I found myself in Alcacer do Sal talking to the public prosecutor. He said to me:

"There is great anxiety in the town. People are afraid that the murderer may choose another victim. At night-time every house is bolted and locked and the slightest sound creates alarm."

"Fingerprints of the dead man were taken, I hope?"

"Yes, I have them here."

"Good. I'll arrange for them to be checked in Lisbon. Now, I want to see the shepherd who found the body."

We went out to the farm and found the shepherd, a very shy and simple fellow. He took us to the spot where he had discovered the body. It was in a barren field and he pointed to a great ilex tree. "He was lying under that tree and I first saw him very early in the morning before the sun had risen," explained the shepherd. "A coat covered the top part of his body and he seemed to be sleeping.

"Some hours later I passed near to him again. He did not seem to have moved at all, and by then the sun was high in the sky and blazing down on him. It seemed strange to me that he should remain there in the fierce heat, and I went over and said: 'Wake up, if you don't want to get roasted.' He never moved, so I pulled the coat away and saw a sight I shall never forget."

The shepherd began to sway on his feet and covered his face with his hands.

"Go on," I insisted. "Tell me what you saw."

"The man had no head, senhor. Above his shirt was nothing but a black mass of blood. It was horrible!"

A few farm labourers had gone with us to the ilex tree, and I turned to them and asked if they knew of anyone who had disappeared from the neighbourhood recently. It was a question none of them could answer, but the youngest of them said: "The murdered man might be one of two men I saw walking across a field near here on the evening before he was found."

I wanted to know what they looked like, and the young labourer said they were strangers to him. One was tall and the other much smaller, and each carried a haversack and scythe.

"Many come here from all parts for the harvesting," explained the shepherd, and then one of the men said a local farmer named Silvestre had given two men a lift on the day prior to the murder.

Silvestre lived in a village near by, and he told me that on June 20th he had given two men a lift in his cart. His description agreed with the one given by the young labourer.

"The tall one," said Silvestre, "was very talkative and told me that he and his companion had been working at Ferreira do Alentejo, which, as you know, senhor, is a hundred and fifty-five kilometres south-east of here, and were returning home. He told me his name was Manuel dos Santos and that he had three children and lived in Odemira in this province."

"Did the other man tell you who he was?"

"No. He was a surly customer and never spoke a word. He just sat in my cart as silent as a mute with his hat over his eyes and his hands clasped behind his head."

The following day I returned to Lisbon and with the fingerprints I had brought from Alcacer do Sal it was quite a simple task to identify the victim as Manuel dos Santos, a fifty-three-year-old widower of Odemira. He was, of course, Farmer Silvestre's "tall man."

I sent a detective to Odemira, but the address on the identity card was closed up and he found dos Santos's seventeen-year-old daughter, Maria Antonia, living with her godparents in the nearby village of Fornos das Fornalhas.

The girl was brought to my office, and it was not a nice thing to have to tell her what had happened to her father. She began to cry, and I waited until she was able to compose herself before asking when she had last heard from him. She handed me two letters. One was of no importance, but the other, dated a few days before his death, had been sent from Beja, which is also in Alentejo province and about 180 kilometres from Lisbon. Manuel dos Santos said he would arrive home after paying a visit to Barreiro (a village on the north bank of the Tagus, opposite Lisbon). He also said he had managed to save 400 escudos and the letter ended "Goodbye . . . goodbye" and appeared to be a strange expression from a man who expected to see his daughter within a few days.

Both letters were written in different hands, and Maria told me that as her father could hardly write at all it was not unusual for him to get one or another of his friends, better educated than himself, to write his letters for him. I asked her if it was customary for him to end his letters by saying "Goodbye" and she said she had never known him to do it before.

As I saw it at the moment, Manuel dos Santos had been murdered for the little money he had been able to save and none was more likely to have killed him than his companion, whom he had asked to write a letter in which, unwittingly, he had provided the motive. The unusual ending to the letter merely expressed the sardonic nature of the killer.

Following a conference at headquarters it was decided to issue a statement to the Press, of which the following is a part:

The identity of the decapitated body found on June 21st on farmland a few kilometres from Alcacer do Sal . . . has now been established as that of Manuel dos Santos, 53, widower and casual farm labourer of Odemira.

Chief Antonio Afonso of the Policia Judiciaria, who is in charge of inquiries, is anxious to interview the companion who was with him on the night before he met his death. This man is lean, swarthy, with a loose beard and short in stature. It is believed he may be in possession of certain information which will prove helpful to the authorities.

Chief Afonso also urgently requests all farmers and farm foremen between Beja and Vendas Novas to send him or public prosecutor Dr. Orlando de Faria Saraiva Lima the names and identity numbers of all men employed by them between June 2nd and June 15th.

On that date dos Santos left for the village of Barreiro. On the evening of June 20th he was seen with a companion in Santa Susana, where he asked a farmer to give them a lift in his cart. . . .

Nothing came of this appeal, and since dos Santos's last letter had been sent from Beja I went there to make some inquiries. Surely somebody would remember him from the two photographs I took along with me—his identity card picture, in which he wore a straggling moustache, and the other clean shaven, as Silvestre had described him.

I did not have much luck at first, but eventually I found someone who said he believed that dos Santos had worked for a foreman named Antonio Pacheco on a farm at Evora. Pacheco, whom I traced easily enough, admitted he had employed dos Santos.

"Why have you not come forward before?" I asked. "Don't you

read the papers? Withholding information from the police is a serious offence."

The foreman was contrite. "Please, senhor, you must forgive me. I am an ignorant fool. I have been working very hard and intended reporting it as soon as the harvest is finished."

Pacheco gave me the names and descriptions of seven men he had employed, and I recognised the man I wanted to meet. His name was Antonio Pereira. The foreman knew very little about him and could not say from where he came.

After a long search six of the men whose names Pacheco had given me were traced, and all of them gave a satisfactory explanation of their whereabouts between the early evening of June 20th and four o'clock the next morning. None of them could tell me anything about Antonio Pereira, except that he was a companion of the murdered man and a dour character who never spoke about himself.

"It seems that nobody knows where Pereira can be found," said my assistant as the last of our witnesses departed.

"A man who keeps so quiet about himself must have had a lot to hide," I replied. "Let us not forget either that anybody callous enough to decapitate his victim is probably a hardened criminal. He may have a record in one or another of the criminal registers. Let's try Evora first."

It was a good guess, and we found that our quarry had been indicted on two charges of robbery. The register gave his last known address as Quinta do Sousa, ao Djebe, in Evora. He had been born in Estremoz, was said to be living with a woman named Maria Rosa Garcia, and was the father of her three children.

With Police Officer Samuel and a man named Adamastor, who had worked on the farm at Evora and swore he would be able to identify Pereira, I went to the address where he was said to be living. It was a miserable dwelling, terribly dilapidated with patched walls and broken windows.

The woman who answered the door was, I judged, about thirty-five and a slattern whose unkempt hair fell to her shoulders. Clinging to her ragged skirts were three young children—a girl and two boys. All were deformed and they were unable to walk normally, but hopped like young kangaroos. I have never seen more fearsome children.

When I asked the woman if her name was Maria Rosa Garcia she looked at me with eyes that were shifty and full of fear. "What do you want?"

I slipped one foot against the rickety door she held open and replied: "We are police officers and want to speak to Antonio Pereira."

"He is not here and I don't know where he is. What is it you want to see him about?" she asked slyly.

"You'll know soon enough. Out of the way; we are going to search the house."

She allowed us to pass, but the moment we were inside she slipped in front of us, threw herself on the floor and began to scream.

"You can stop that," I said brusquely. "It won't do you any good."

I sent the police officer upstairs to have a look around and then Adamastor pointed to a scythe in the room.

"Look, senhor," he said, "that belonged to Manuel dos Santos. I recognise it as his because of its long blade. I tried it myself while he was working with us. And those are his finger-covers hanging on the wall. He was the only one among us who had covers made of leather."

Samuel came downstairs with two pairs of trousers, all that he had been able to find. Adamastor's eyes lit up again as he pointed to one pair. "They belonged to dos Santos. I saw him wearing them."

We took the woman to the local police station for questioning, and there she made a startling confession. She was not Pereira's mistress in the ordinary sense, but his sister. The deformed children had been born out of their incestuous passion. Her name was Lucinda Pereira, not Maria Rosa Garcia, but she could not tell us where we could find her brother. At least, that is what she said.

A general call to every police department was made for the arrest of Pereira, and, in the meantime, I asked officials at Estremoz, his birthplace, to forward any information that was available about the family. It seems that the document that had to be signed when Antonio Pereira was born had to await his father's release from jail. The old man was a notorious thief known as "The Wolf's Hand." He was the head of a gang of robbers and housebreakers and he was joined by his son as soon as he was old enough. When the gang was smashed most of its members were deported to Portuguese East Africa, where the father died. Antonio himself returned to Portugal after spending eleven years in a penal settlement.

In a further interrogation Lucinda Pereira confessed that on July

17th, a week before her arrest, she had received 700 escudos from her brother with which she paid off debts. This was in addition to 400 escudos he had sent her about the end of June. It told us that even if Antonio Pereira had been in regular work from the time he was seen with dos Santos by Silvestre and up to the second occasion when he sent his sister more money that he could not possibly have saved 1,100 escudos.

On July 25th, thirty-four days after the murder of Manuel dos Santos, every newspaper throughout Portugal carried a photograph of Pereira and a description: "Medium build, lean, dark in colouring, tanned by the sun, has a loose beard and a thin, angular face. Anyone seeing this man is asked to communicate immediately with police headquarters in Lisbon."

He was arrested a few days later. A patrol of the Republican National Guard picked him up while he was on his knees roasting a chicken in a coppice. When told he was wanted for the murder of Manuel dos Santos, he at first denied all knowledge of the crime, but later said he had killed his companion in self-defence.

"We quarrelled," he said. "He went for me like a mad dog, crying out that he would kill me. To save my life I had to destroy him."

He was taken under close escort to the Tribunal at Alcacer do Sal, where I interrogated him. At first he would not budge from his story, explaining that he had severed dos Santos's head in order to prevent identification.

"I was frightened that if the police found out who he was they would trace his killing to me, and it would be difficult for me to explain the truth. I had no witness to prove my words."

"Did you not realise we should be able to identify the dead man by his fingerprints?" I queried.

"No, I did not think of that," mumbled Pereira.

"I think you are lying," I said. "You killed dos Santos after learning from the letter you wrote for him to his daughter that he had saved four hundred escudos. He was a bigger man than you, stronger, too, and the only chance you had to get hold of the money was to kill him."

Pereira's face became ashen. "It is not true," he cried. "We quarrelled, not about money but about a woman, and fought. If I had not killed him by hitting him over the head with a stick he would have killed me. It was my life or his."

"Did you write a letter for him to his daughter while you were both in Beja?" I asked.

"Yes, senhor, I admit I did." There was saliva at the corners of his mouth.

"And did you finish it by writing the words 'Goodbye . . . good-bye'?"

"Yes, yes, senhor. That also is true."

"Why?"

"Because he told me to write them."

"Even though he expected to see his daughter in a few days? People don't usually write a final farewell such as that unless there is good reason for doing so."

Going to a cupboard in the room, I took out the coat which had been found over Manuel dos Santos's body.

"Take a look at this," I said, turning the coat inside out. The lining was badly stained with blood and particles of human hair still adhered to the material.

Pereira gripped the rail of a chair to steady himself. He closed his eyes as though to shut out the sight of the coat.

"Shall I tell you what really occurred?" I asked him. "Manuel dos Santos put it over his head when he decided to take a nap under the ilex tree. It was evening and he was very tired. You waited until he was asleep, then hit him over the head until he was dead. Look!" I cried, holding the coat up close to Pereira. "His blood has saturated the lining and there are still strands of his hair on it."

"All—right," he said painfully. "It—was—like—that."

"What did you do with the head?"

He said he had wrapped it in a piece of packing-cloth and buried it in a thicket of brambles.

At his trial at Alcacer do Sal, Antonio Lopes Pereira, forty-two, a confirmed and hardened criminal by any reckoning, was sentenced to ten years' imprisonment followed by twenty years in a penal settlement. At his age, a life sentence could hardly have been more severe.

For her immoral way of living and harbouring the criminal, Lucinda Pereira, his sister, was sent to prison for two and a half years, or alternatively to three years and nine months in a detention settlement.

Both heard their fate without any sign of emotion.

Too Smart to be Clever

by Vedat Sokullu, Chief of Murder Department, Security Directory of Istanbul, Turkey

THOSE WHO DIE peacefully in their beds, with all their affairs left in good order, are indeed among the favoured.

It was not the destiny of Abdurrahman Bozkurt to die quietly, his passing watched by his family and friends. His end was violent and he breathed his last moments face downwards on the floor of a basement lavatory in a warehouse in the Harbiye district of Istanbul.

The warehouse was occupied by the State Monopoly Administration and Bozkurt was the night watchman there. He was fifty-six years old and not very robust. Those who knew him liked his quiet ways and occasional smile.

It was one of his friends who discovered the murder on the night of January 13th, 1956. As he was passing the warehouse he saw the door was open and that the streaming light of a single bulb shone from the corridor of the general office. He thought it likely that Bozkurt had forgotten to close the door, and had fallen asleep, and he went inside to arouse him. The door of the office was ajar and he looked inside. It was sparsely furnished with an ordinary desk, a couple of bentwood chairs and a safe that stood in one of the corners. On the floor lay a screwdriver and a gleaming adze. There were also spots of blood around and the signs of a struggle—a chair knocked over and a metal tray and its contents brushed from the desk.

Alarmed, Bozkurt's friend followed a trail of blood from the office along the corridor, and down the stairs to the basement, where he found the body of the battered watchman sprawled on the floor of the lavatory. In the presence of murder the searcher suddenly turned and fled along the way he had come. As soon as he reached the street, he ran to where he knew he would find a police officer.

My wife and I were just preparing for bed when news of the crime was telephoned to me. I picked up a taxi and when I arrived at the warehouse a police surgeon was examining the body. Bozkurt was still alive, he explained, when his body was dumped in the basement. He had suffered severe head injuries from a sharp-edged weapon and death had taken place some time between ten and eleven o'clock. Two fingerprint experts and a photographer were waiting for me to have a look round before starting work themselves.

The safe in the office was scratched and marked with small indentations made by someone who had tried to force it open by using the adze and screwdriver. The attempt was clumsy and ineffectual, as it was bound to be, and obviously was the work of an amateur. All the signs were there to be read; Bozkurt had disturbed the intruder while he was trying to open the safe. It would not have been difficult to have overpowered the old man, but, instead, he had been murdered, probably because his assailant was well known to him.

Anybody accustomed to visiting the warehouse would be likely to know that money taken after the banks were closed was kept in the safe until the following day.

The killer, it seemed, had worn gloves. There were no fingerprints on the screwdriver or adze or, for that matter, on the safe or door of the office.

In one of the drawers of the desk we found a notebook containing the name and address of the director of the warehouse and I sent a police car for him. He had never seen the adze and screwdriver before and was certain they did not belong to anyone who worked on the premises.

The following morning we picked up a bit of information about Bozkurt. He was last seen alive at a nearby café where, in fact, he went every night for a cup of coffee and a piece of bread. Usually he stayed about twenty minutes and did not trouble to lock the door of the warehouse.

"I often spoke to him about it," said the café proprietor, "and told him that one night he would suffer for his carelessness. 'You'll go back and find someone there up to no good,' I would say to him jokingly, and he would reply: 'Never fear, they'll get more than they bargain for.' "

"Did he ever come here with anyone?" asked one of my detectives.

"No. He was always alone, as he was last night, poor fellow."

It was evident that the killer knew of the old man's nightly visits to the café. He had waited for him to leave and had then slipped into the warehouse to rob the safe. He could not open it and Bozkurt had returned to meet his death.

We did not want such tracks as were left to grow cold, and, for the next three days and nights, every detective in the murder squad was recruited in a combined effort to run down the killer. We found the shop where the adze and screwdriver had been bought, but nobody could tell us anything about the purchaser.

"We sell too many of them to remember faces," said the salesman.

Petty crooks and other doubtful characters known to us were pulled in for questioning. So were street-walkers, but they, too, had nothing to say and it was not long before we were facing a barrage from the newspapers for our failure. In one editorial we were described with poetic irony as "flowers of the field, who toil not, neither do they spin, yet Solomon in all his glory was not arrayed like one of these."

One act in the murder of Abdurrahman Bozkurt puzzled me. It was hard to understand why the killer had dragged the body of his unconscious and dying victim along a forty-foot corridor, down a flight of stairs and into the lavatory. Why not leave him in the office where he had been struck down?

I believed I knew the explanation, and that night went back to the warehouse to re-enact the crime under conditions similar to those in which it had taken place. Two burly policemen, smart in blue-grey uniforms, and each armed with a service revolver, were on guard at the entrance. I took one of them inside with me to play the part of the watchman.

"Now," I said, getting on my knees to face the safe in the office, "you have come back from the café to find me here tampering with the safe and you cry out: 'Hey, you, what do you think you are doing?'

"I swing round immediately and you at once recognise me. You call out my name and I try to push past you, but you throw your arms around me to prevent me from leaving. We struggle and I punch you

in the face and you fall over. Before you can get to your feet I snatch
up the adze and bring it down on your head, just like this." I described a movement with my clenched fist that descended on the
police officer's skull and he, playing his part accordingly, rolled over
on the floor. " 'Help! Murder!' you cry out as you try to ward off the
attack. I bring down the adze on your head again and then again
and you are no longer capable of crying out. I can tell by your heavy
breathing that you are unconscious." I pushed the officer over on his
side and asked him: "What then is my next move?"

He got up on his haunches, his eyes bright with excitement. "You
are incapable of thinking very clearly and uncertain if the watchman
is dying or just knocked out. If he comes to, you don't want him calling out, so you have to put him where he can't be heard. You are
familiar with the warehouse and so you drag him down to the basement and to the lavatory there."

"First rate!" I replied. "You have a lively mind. But there is more
to it than that. The killer was suddenly struck with what he thought
was a brilliant idea—smart beyond all words. Come, we will see if
my theory is correct."

We hurried along the corridor and down the short flight of stairs
to the water-closet. The place had been locked up since the night of
the murder, but I had retained the key. I opened the door.

My hand found the switch just inside, but as I pulled down the
little porcelain dolly no light came on. I took a torch out of my pocket
and directed its beam to the pendant hanging from a short length
of flex from the ceiling. There was a bulb there right enough. It
could have blown or there might be a faulty connection. I tested the
switch, but there was nothing wrong there, and I then stood on the
lavatory seat to take a closer look at the bulb. It was not firm in its
holder and that was why it was impossible to switch on the light.

"I believe I know what has happened," I said to the police officer,
who was looking up at me. "Remember I told you that there was
something the killer suddenly thought of and which he believed was
awfully smart?"

"I remember you saying so, sir."

"Well, I'll tell you what it was. He wanted to guard against the
possibility of Bozkurt regaining consciousness and reaching for the
light switch. He knew he had gravely injured the watchman, and it
seemed a Machiavellian trick to him to ensure that if Bozkurt opened

his eyes it would be the terror of darkness that would bring closer the onset of death."

The police officer looked puzzled and I anticipated the question he was going to ask me. "Yes, it would have been far easier to make sure of Bozkurt's death rather than go to all this trouble. But murderers, as my long experience has taught me, often do strange things. They can just as easily be in the grip of vanity no less than panic, and in moments of crisis an idea occurs to them that they imagine is a master-stroke. If my theory is the right one, we shall have the fingerprints of the killer on the bulb."

"But, sir—if you will pardon my interrupting you—isn't the killer supposed to have worn gloves?"

"Yes, he did. But they had become soaked in the blood of his victim, and, to dislodge the bulb enough to break the contact, he had to take them off."

"Why not remove the bulb completely?"

This officer had an inquiring mind and he was to be admired. "As I have said already, a murderer's actions are not dictated by the logic of normal persons. That is too much to expect. One must never be surprised by an action that seems unaccountable. Hand me your knife and then go and turn off the current at the main. I am going to cut down this light pendant."

A little later I was back at my office at the Security Directory. I put on a pair of rubber gloves and fitted the bulb I had brought from the warehouse into the socket of my desk lamp. The bulb lit up and I could see that the faint smudges on its surface were fingerprints. I sent the bulb down to the laboratory for pictures to be taken of the fingerprints, and when they had been developed I handed them over to Muhsin Bach, an officer of long experience in the fingerprints section.

"Take a look at these," I said. "I believe they belong to the man who killed Abdurrahman Bozkurt. If you can match them it will be the end of our search."

The fingerprints were first checked against those of persons with recent convictions and also with everyone employed at the warehouse. None of these matched, and for the next four days hundreds of fingerprints were scrutinised not only of persons of criminal tendencies, but of those taken during the issue of passports and traffic licences. I did not doubt that if the murderer's fingerprints had been taken at some time or another we should be able to find him, but there was always a possibility that we were searching for something we did not possess.

Then, ninety-six hours afterwards, my secretary hurried into my room and burst out: "They want you in the fingerprints department. I think they have found what they were looking for." It was January 25th, exactly twelve days after the discovery of the crime.

I found Muhsin Bach bending over a table littered with cards and records. "We've got him," he cried, and pointed to the photographs taken from the bulb and a set belonging to the police records.

"His name is Ismet Erich," said Bach. "He is a young man and not long ago was arrested on a charge of gambling. It was nothing very serious and he had not been in trouble before. Quite by chance we took his fingerprints, and we would have found them earlier had the file on him not been closed. Take a look, Chief, his fingerprints tally in every detail with those on the bulb."

Bach was not a person given to exaggerating and he had secured a perfect match. "You've done a good job," I said. "Who is the bird, and what do we know of him?"

"He lives, or did at the time he was picked up, at Sishli, in Ferikoy Street, in some flats owned by his father. He gave his occupation as that of a car driver."

Sishli is a residential district of Istanbul and a thirty minutes' drive from the centre of the city. Two officers accompanied me when we drove out there to have a talk with Ismet Erich. We found the block of flats owned by his father, but did not seek him out at once. Opposite the building there was a small grocery and delicatessen store and we went over and asked the proprietor if he knew young Ismet Erich. He nodded.

"He is a very handsome young man, as any girl round here will tell you. He is married, dresses very smartly and is fond of driving his car at top speed. I believe his father is very generous to him. Ismet, though, is an inveterate gambler. Owing to the shortage of lines there is not a telephone at his home, and his friends with whom he gambles at cards frequently ring up here for him. Ismet always tips my boy well when he runs over to tell him that there is a call for him."

The grocer knew who we were and, at my suggestion, he sent his boy with a message that Ismet Erich was wanted on the telephone.

After a few moments we saw him leave the building opposite and walk over. He had a strong-looking face, somewhat saturnine, curly black hair and moustache and very dark eyes. I could well imagine the girls falling for him. He was very smartly dressed and looked, if anything, a little older than the twenty-eight years our records said he was. As he entered the shop, I stepped forward and the two officers with me closed in on him.

"Ismet Erich, I am a police officer," I explained, "and I have reason to believe you were concerned with the killing of Abdurrahman Bozkurt, a night watchman at a warehouse in Harbiye. I must ask you to accompany us to the Security Directory, where I shall put certain questions to you."

Erich's mouth tightened and his eyes narrowed and I thought he would try to bolt. He looked round and saw the other officers, and I could see how dismayed he was. He turned to me again and his expressive eyes looked as if they were beseeching me. Suddenly he put his hands to his face and began to weep.

We took him back with us to the Security Directory, and in the presence of Chief of Police Hayredding Nakiboglu he made a full confession. Here it is, as I recorded it in my notebook.

"Gambling has destroyed me. For gambling I sold my car only to leave my last *kurush* [penny] in a gambling den on New Year's night. I was newly married and feared to cause my wife unhappiness. I had to get money somehow because I wanted to buy back my car. I could not ask my father for so much. Thinking of how I could get the money, I remembered the safe in the State Monopoly warehouse. I had frequently taken goods there in the daytime and knew that large sums were often locked up in the office safe for the night. I decided to make this my last gamble.

"For several nights I watched the place, studying the movements and habits of the old watchman. When I noticed that every time he went to the little café he left open the door of the warehouse the job seemed to be easy. I bought a screwdriver and an adze, thinking that these tools would be sufficient to open the safe. What a fool I was to imagine that the safe could be forced with them. Just as I was thinking of giving it up as a bad job the old man came back. He knew me at once."

Erich described how he struggled with Bozkurt and then hit him with the adze, before dragging him senseless to the water-closet so that his cries could not be heard from the street.

"I meant him to die because he had recognised me and would have told the police about me. I thought he might die quicker shut up in the pitch darkness of the closet, so I loosened the electric light bulb. Why I troubled to do that I cannot say. It was stupid and unnecessary. If I had not removed my gloves, which were saturated with blood, I would not have left my fingerprints and you would never have caught me."

After a long and tedious trial Ismet Erich was found guilty of the murder of the watchman and sentenced to death by the First Criminal Court at Istanbul.

At the moment of writing he is in the Sultanahmet Prison awaiting the decision of the Court of Appeal.

Murderer in Mufti

by Shigeo Chiba, Chief of the C.I.D.,
East Sendai, Japan

H E WAS a big man—over six feet, broad and with powerful shoulders, a stubborn chin and ice-blue eyes that warned you the weather was invariably chilly. The silver eagles on the epaulettes of his gaberdine tunic denoted his colonelcy, and he was, in fact, Commandant of a big United States army camp at East Sendai, a provincial town on the east coast of Japan, two hundred miles from Tokyo.

When he walked into my office I could see from his scowl that he was a man with a mission. He was here to raise hell, and would not leave before he had done so. Many Japanese plays have this situation—it is called the confrontation scene and is a test of will between two characters, and very thrilling if you are in the audience.

"Good morning, Commandant," I said, greeting him with a bow. "I am happy to welcome you to police headquarters."

"You'll not be so goddam happy when I've finished with you," he replied in a mid-West drawl that was not entirely musical even by Western standards. "Another of my boys took a beating up last night, and that, Chiba, makes the twentieth in three months."

I knew the figures just as well as he did, because from the very first moment these attacks on American servicemen began I had done my best to put a stop to them. Many of the men spent their evenings in Sendai's unsavoury bars and dives, and, invariably, were stewed and befuddled when they staggered out of these places to return to camp. In most instances the pattern was the same—they had been clubbed into insensibility and robbed of their money and possessions without even catching a glimpse of their assailant. There were a few cases, though, in which the men admitted they had been lured into a dark alley by a painted Japanese girl. Instead of the sexual gratification they had anticipated, they had been knocked out and rolled for their money.

The United States army authorities were convinced that these vicious assaults were carried out by a Japanese, in fact, a *goto,* the name by which a footpad is known in Japan. I was being looked askance at because I had not yet got him under lock and key.

And, clearly, it was my task to find the wretch. Under an agreement between the respective governments of America and Japan, criminal jurisdiction over United States soldiers in our country had been divided since 1952. The American authorities tried their own men for any crime committed at their bases or while the men were on duty. Any offence that took place away from the service camps when the men were off duty, including those involving the Japanese themselves, became the concern of our civil administration. In this way the assaults had become my problem.

Every Japanese police officer on patrol had been told to pick up any likely suspect and to watch the roads from Sendai back to camp, but there had been nothing to report and nobody to interrogate. All we knew was that the wanted man was uncannily wise to the habits and routine of servicemen. The attacks occurred often on short cuts back to the camp and, invariably, on the evenings of pay days. I set up special patrols at these points, but with no luck. As soon as the watchers were switched elsewhere another man would be beaten up. Now the twentieth attack had taken place and the Commandant had come to tell me what he thought of Japanese police methods.

"This boy—Corporal Edward K. Maunakea, from Honolulu, is in a bad way," he stormed. "Likely enough he's going to peg out. That's the opinion of the hospital doctor. He was violently clubbed and robbed of fifty dollars a mile from camp. He came to and crawled back to camp bleeding from the ears and nose. He passed out and is still unconscious."

"It's a terrible thing," I said.

"Terrible!" replied the Commandant edgily. "Hell, that's a cute understatement. This can turn out to be murder. Understand, Chiba, murder? If this boy dies I want one of your Japs for first-degree murder."

"Look, Commandant, I don't like these attacks any more than you do, but I cannot help thinking that we may be looking for the wrong person. It is not absolutely certain that it is the work of a Japanese."

"Listen, you've given me that spiel before. What makes you think the bastard isn't a Jap?"

"It is, I admit, just a feeling I have got about these cases. You will agree, surely, that for a Japanese he knows a great deal about army routine—the time the men are paid, where they drink, and the many routes back to camp."

The Commandant pushed the idea aside. "These aren't secrets, and what goes on in the normal way could be found out by anyone. Get this, robbery is the sole motive for the assaults, and if you believe it is one of our own boys I should advise you to think again. The American army is well paid and our fellows don't have to rob one another to get their hands on some dough."

"Do you remember telling me not long after this business first began about one of your coloured soldiers deserting?"

"You mean Private Orvis Boone, who broke out of detention barracks last April while serving a short sentence for fighting in camp?"

"Yes, that was the man. Did you ever find him?"

"No, we did not. He vanished completely, even though we had the military police looking for him. We decided he had gone south towards Tokyo or maybe Yokohama. Could be he has left the country. Boone isn't your bird, Chiba; don't count on him."

The Commandant got up to go, and as a parting shot he said: "Don't I wish I had somebody from the F.B.I. here. They would have grabbed him, wherever he was."

Two days later the Commandant telephoned to say that Corporal Maunakea had died the previous night from cerebral haemorrhage.

"Never regained consciousness," he said grimly. "Now you've got a murder case on your hands, Chiba, and this calls for results. Uncle Sam wants the hide of the sonofabitch who killed Maunakea."

The voice crackled on the diaphragm of the instrument like storm signals on a radio set. I put down the telephone quietly and tried to think how it was possible to lay my hands on a wraith.

But as startlingly as they had begun the assaults suddenly ceased, and as the days slipped by the possibility grew stronger that the last had been heard of them. It was quite likely, I thought, that the death of Corporal Maunakea had so badly frightened his killer that he had left Sendai altogether. We still wanted him, but if he had disappeared the affair had, to that extent, passed out of my hands. We had not even a description to offer to police elsewhere.

We did not forget, of course, or abandon our quest, and six quiet and orderly weeks followed each other until the night we found a body in the smoking embers of a gutted house on the edge of the town, not very far from the camp. This time the victim was a pretty girl of twenty-four.

Fires are greatly feared in Japan because houses are mostly made of light matchwood and there is always a danger of an entire town being engulfed from a single outbreak. The penalty for arson is the same as for murder, and even negligence is a punishable offence.

Almost every fire that takes place is investigated by the police, and that was why I went out in the early hours of a September morning to look at what remained of the house (which had been partly occupied by Miss Kikuko Muraki) after a fire which, apparently, had cost the young woman her life. The body was unrecognisable, but there was no doubt whose it was.

Miss Muraki, very personable and vivacious, was a waitress and had been the mistress of a coloured serviceman stationed at the camp. She had rented two rooms at the house to be near him. The couple had decided to get married in a month's time and had planned to make their home in America. According to neighbours they were very much in love, and nobody had heard so much as a cross word between them.

On the night of the fire Miss Muraki's fiancé visited her and was seen to leave the house about midnight to return to camp. How the fire had begun nobody could say.

Later that morning Miss Muraki's landlord, her closest neighbour and friend, said that only a few days before the girl had bought a new bicycle that she kept in the house. There was no trace of it among the blackened remains and it certainly could not have been wholly destroyed by the fire.

I wanted to know what had happened to the machine and a search was made, but it was nowhere to be found. Miss Muraki's friends and acquaintances were questioned, but could tell us no more than we knew already. She was well liked and there was no history of enmity or quarrels. Nevertheless the post-mortem examination revealed that Miss Muraki's death was not due to the fire. She had been so violently strangled that her neck was broken and her killer had then set fire to the house to obliterate the crime.

It did not seem feasible that robbery was the motive. The girl possessed neither money nor jewels of her own, although, of course, her fiancé might have given her some cash to look after. Most soldiers, as was known, left their spare cash with the bank which was attached to the camp. As likely as not, the theft of the bicycle was an afterthought.

I wondered if jealousy could have inspired the murder, but it was a theory disputed by the facts. Miss Muraki had been eager to marry her Negro and everybody swore she had given him no reason to doubt her faithfulness. If it was a crime of passion it was not her fiancé who had committed it. We had been able to establish that the girl was alive when he left her that night, and we knew he had reached the camp in good time and had stayed there. Could there be another man—somebody who had knocked at Miss Muraki's door when her lover had gone?

Thinking over the problem in the quiet of my office I recalled, for no especial reason—at least it seemed so—reading an account of an American Negro soldier who, some time before, had spent his leave working on a farm near to the village of Shikano, which is some distance from Sendai. The people of the village had called him the "gentle American farmer." He was a man of impressive build and great strength and could handle a truss of hay as if it were child's play.

I began to understand why I had remembered this "gentle American," as he was called. Miss Muraki liked Negroes, as did indeed many Japanese, and there was no reason why she should not have known more than one. The man who had killed her had used great violence that sprang from great strength.

It was possible that I was chasing a blind hare, but I decided it was worth the trouble to pay a visit to the village. I could not remember if the paper had published the man's name.

The villagers had not forgotten the gentle American. "A very nice person and a fine worker. We were sorry when he left."

"What was his name?" I asked.

"We never rightly knew," answered a man who had worked with him. "We used to call him Sammy. He was about six feet and talked and moved slowly, but he was a tireless worker. I have never seen anyone whose hands were so massive. They were half as big again as mine, and I am supposed to have large hands."

I was able to get a very good description of this unknown Negro, and on my return to Sendai I had one of my assistants write it out clearly and carefully in English so that I could take it to the camp and show it to the Commandant.

I gave it to him and said: "It may recall somebody to you or to the other officers in the camp."

He read the description very carefully and then looked at me with his ice-blue eyes. "Say!" he exclaimed. "This seems to fit Private Orvis Boone, you know, the Negro who took a run-out powder from here. I'd like to know how you came across this description."

I told him about my trip to Shikano and could not resist adding: "Your deserter might not, after all, have gone to Tokyo or Yokohama as was thought. It's too early to be certain, but I shall not be surprised if he is not far from Sendai."

"Yeah," the Commandant said thoughtfully. "You know something, Chiba? The medical evidence suggests that from the situation of many of the wounds some of my boys were bludgeoned by a tall person, and Boone fills the bill in this respect."

He walked up and down the room with his hands thrust deep in his pockets. "I wonder where he is?" he said more to himself than to me. "Not in Shikano, otherwise you would have known. Tell you what," he said in a decisive manner, "I'll have a dragnet thrown over the whole area. What d'you say?"

"For the moment I would rather you did not. I have other inquiries to make and I will let you know immediately I have any news."

I had considered before the possibility of Kikuko Muraki being the victim of jealousy. Perhaps she had known Boone before she had fallen in love with the soldier she had agreed to marry. Boone may have wanted to return to her and found she would have nothing more to do with him. It would explain the ferocious attack on the poor girl.

I had another talk with her landlord. I described Boone to him and asked him if he remembered whether Miss Muraki was at any time friendly with such a man.

"Yes, I think I know who it is," he answered. "He used to visit Miss Muraki in company with Shigeko Sasaki, a young person with whom he was associating. She was not a girl of good character and Miss Muraki told me that this girl had come to Sendai from Shikano to attend school. She had, however, got into vicious company. I am sure she had become the mistress of the man you have described. I am sorry, but I never heard his name."

"Have you seen them here lately?"

"No, not for some time."

I was now able to work on firmer ground than before, and I mobilised every available police officer to search Sendai for an American and a Japanese girl who would be living together, probably in a small room in some place or other. They were traced quite easily—to a shack on the far side of a stream and close to the ricefields. It was less than four hundred yards from the house where Miss Muraki had met her death.

"I am certain it's the couple you want. He doesn't wear a uniform and is not seen about in the daytime," reported the detective who had found them.

"Keep them under observation and don't let them out of your sight," I said.

I rang up the Commandant and gave him the news. "Good for you, Chiba," he said. "I'll bring some military police along and together we'll pick them up."

At dusk we had the shack surrounded. "The girl has been out once, but she has returned," said my detective. "I haven't seen the man, but you'll find him in there."

Four of us, three hefty military police and myself, approached the door very quietly and stood listening for a moment. We could hear the couple talking the pidgin talk of both languages.

I flung open the door, and they looked up in astonishment from the broken-down table at which they were seated. The Negro was naked to the waist and wore a pair of soiled slacks and canvas shoes. In the half light his body glistened and I saw the ripple of muscles as he turned to face us. It was Orvis Boone, and the military police knew him at once.

"You've been gone a long time, bud," said one of them as he

snapped a pair of handcuffs over his huge black wrists. Boone came quietly and so did the girl, but she looked very frightened.

In the shack was Miss Muraki's bicycle and many of the personal belongings of the soldiers who had been beaten up and robbed. Boone confessed that he had killed Miss Muraki.

He said that he and Shigeko Sasaki wanted money from her and had hidden among the trees near her house until they saw her fiancé leave. They had then called on her, but she had refused to hand anything over because she needed all her money for her wedding. Boone became enraged, grabbed her by the throat to frighten her into handing over the cash and said he had broken her neck, unintentionally.

"I never meant to kill," he said in a husky voice. "I jes' wanted to make her hand over her dough. She sure had plenty. That guy she was goin' to marry gave her every cent he got. Yessir! But I guess ma girl friend egged me on. 'Better kill her and take all she has,' she said to me. 'If you don't, she'll tell the cops an' they'll get you.' Yessir! That's what she said. So I guess I kinda pressed her throat until she was dead."

There were contradictions in this statement, because if Boone had accidentally killed Miss Muraki by a too free display of his great strength how was it that Shigeko Sasaki had found it necessary to incite him to kill her?

In the women's prison at Sendai the girl admitted that she had been with Boone but passionately denied that she had urged him to kill Miss Muraki.

"He lies," she cried with flashing eyes. "I tried to stop him, but he was so big and strong and mad with temper, I could do nothing. He set fire to the house so that people would think it was an accident."

They had hidden in the shack afterwards and were waiting a chance to leave the district for ever. They intended to get out of the country and enter China.

We got to know what had happened previously. When Boone escaped from detention he had gone with the Sasaki girl to her parents' home in Shikano. He had pretended to be a soldier on leave, and, to get hold of a little money, he had done some work on the farm. He did not reveal his name to anyone and the villagers called him Sammy.

The newspaper story about himself—the "gentle American farmer"—convinced him that it was no longer safe to remain in the village, and he returned with Sasaki to Sendai. It was at this stage that the assaults on servicemen began, for the pair wanted money to leave Japan, and the plan was to rob drunken soldiers. Boone admitted he had clubbed Corporal Maunakea and taken fifty dollars from his wallet.

For killing Maunakea Private Orvis L. C. Boone, aged twenty-three, of Texas, and serving in the United States Army First Cavalry Division (Fifth Regimental Combat Team) was first tried by court martial and sentenced to imprisonment for life.

He was then handed over to the Japanese civil authorities and with Shigeko Sasaki tried for murder, arson and robbery. Judge Mizuo Yamada described the murder of Miss Muraki as a premeditated atrocity against a trusting friend and a crime that was the most cruel any human being could perpetrate. The judge said further that both defendants were unrepentant and blamed each other. But both were, nevertheless, willing partners. He sentenced each to death by hanging.

Boone was the first American soldier to receive the death sentence in a Japanese court since the agreement made with Washington in 1952.

His fellow prisoner staggered when she heard her sentence and began to weep. Since the end of the second world war only one woman has ever been hanged in Japan.

Crucifixion in the Jungle

by Deputy Inspector-General of Police G.A.K.
Rockwood, Colombo, Ceylon

THE BIGGEST racing coup ever to be pulled off in Colombo took place not on the well-known racecourse at Havelock Park, but in the streets of Ceylon's capital itself. The result:

(1) Ferocious murder of a native chauffeur.
(2) Theft of £40,000 (four lakhs of rupees) belonging to Colombo's Turf Club.
(3) Company cashier shot and seriously wounded.

The murder preceded the robbery by about fourteen hours, but first let me relate the facts in the order that we ourselves became acquainted with them.

To begin with, the race meetings at Havelock Park are held on the afternoons of each Saturday and at that time the day's receipts were locked up in the company's safe over the weekend, during which the racecourse offices were under guard.

Every Monday morning a car to take the cash to the bank was supplied by Armstrong's Garage. It was invariably a seven-seater limousine driven by a man named John Silva. He was fifty-six, Armstrong's oldest employee, and a man of excellent character.

On Monday morning, January 27th, 1947, there was a change in the routine, and it can be best explained by the injured cashier, whom I talked to in hospital a few hours after the robbery.

"It was much the same as any other Monday morning," said the injured man. "The car from Armstrong's drew up in the usual place outside the offices of the Turf Club at about half-past eight. I saw that Silva, the regular driver, was not at the wheel and I thought that he might, perhaps, be ill. In any case there was a police officer (so I thought) in the seat beside the new driver—as there is every week.

"I saw the trunk containing cheques and the bulk of the cash put into the car and I then got in with my two assistants. The rest of the money was carried in padlocked satchels by three other club employees to the club van, since there was not room for all of us in the car."

"This was the weekly routine?" I asked.

"Absolutely."

"Go on, tell me what happened next."

"Well, I noticed the driver of our car appeared to be in a greater hurry than usual. He did not wait for the van and started up at once. We had not been long on the way when we ran into a traffic jam and that cut us off completely from the van. At the roundabout farther down the road, our driver turned to the right. I told him he should have gone straight on and he said he was sorry. Rather than reverse, he said, he would get back to the main road at the first opportunity. The officer sitting next to him smiled reassuringly and everything seemed all right.

"Shortly afterwards we turned left and I thought the driver was doubling back to reach the regular route. There was, of course, no sign of the van and I assumed we should find it waiting for us outside the bank.

"Our car suddenly slowed down and two men leapt on each running-board. Before I could realise what was taking place I found myself staring into the barrel of a revolver pointed at me by the man I had thought was a police officer. 'Get out or I'll shoot,' he said.

"Both doors of the car were pulled open by the men on the running-boards and they overpowered my colleagues and dragged them out. The man with the gun tried to grab me, but I fought back. I was hanging on to the frame of the door and shouting for help when someone took a flying kick at my hand and broke my grip. I then heard the sound of a shot and everything went black."

The outline of the plot became clearer from what I heard from the manager of Armstrong's Garage. He said that shortly before eight o'clock he had received a telephone call, purportedly from somebody at the Turf Club, to say that the car would not be required that morning until ten o'clock as the receipts had not yet been balanced.

"I had not the slightest suspicion that the call was not genuine. A little after 9 a.m. I rang the club on another matter and before putting down the receiver I confirmed the new arrangement about the car. I was told the car had arrived at the usual time and I then knew something was wrong. I drove round to the offices of the Turf Club, and was talking to the manager when we heard about the robbery."

"What happened to John Silva, the regular driver? Did you tell him about this new arrangement?"

"No. He did not turn up for work this morning and I have not heard from him. He may be ill."

"Was he on duty yesterday?"

"As a matter of fact he was the only driver here. Two men called and said they wanted a big car to take them to Puttalam, which, as you know, is over eighty miles away. It was a job for Silva and he took the saloon car that we use for the Turf Club."

"The same car that the hold-up gang used?"

"Yes, or one similar. "

A detective I had sent to Silva's home returned at this moment. "He has not been home all night, Chief," he told me. "They don't know where he is."

I looked at the manager and said: "It doesn't look too good for your man, does it? As far as we can tell nobody has seen or heard of him since he left for Puttalam, yet at eight-thirty this morning the car with another driver and bogus police officer turns up at the Turf Club. It must have been the same car otherwise the cashier would have noticed it."

"Not if the car was a similar model," corrected the manager.

"The hiring of the car yesterday was part of the hold-up plot. They had to have it to pull off the coup."

"Then what's happened to Silva? It's unthinkable that he was in the plot. He was reliable and trustworthy."

"Money, big and easy money, makes fools of many people," I replied sententiously. "Your trusted chauffeur is no more virtuous than many others in the face of temptation. Four lakhs is a lot of money."

The manager gave me a description of the car and its registration, and my belief that it would soon be found proved right, for it was discovered abandoned a few miles outside Colombo. Nothing had been left behind, but there were several sets of fingerprints which were photographed and passed on to the records department for checking with the files of known criminals.

The man I most wanted to talk to was John Silva. I regarded him as the key figure in the affair. His help had been vital in carrying out the robbery, and, despite his good character, he had fallen for the lure of big money.

The robbery provided the newspapers with a sensational story and ourselves with a new witness. He was the proprietor of a small eating-house at Puttalam and he told us that on Sunday afternoon the saloon car, used in the robbery, had drawn up outside his place. There were four men in it, the driver, an individual who appeared to be some kind of a servant, and two passengers who got out and ordered a meal. They invited the driver to join them and they were very free with the arrack* they drank with their food. They kept filling the glass of the driver.

"Before they had finished," explained the proprietor, "one of them got up and went out. I watched him walk down the road to where a small Standard car was parked. He spoke to whoever was in it and then the car drove off. The man then came back, opened the door of the saloon and told the servant to get out. 'Give him something to eat,' he said to me, 'and please hurry as we want to be on our way.' The servant bolted his food and all of them returned to the car. It drove off northwards, beyond the town where the road turns inland and goes through thick jungle country."

"I don't suppose you had ever seen these men before?"

"No, but I am sure that I could recognise them again. The two passengers were big and powerful-looking men. The servant was somewhat insignificant."

"How about the driver?"

"I remember he looked very hot and tired, as though he had had a hard day. He brightened up after drinking plenty of arrack."

I took a photograph of John Silva from the drawer of my desk and handed it to him.

"Can you tell me who this is?" I asked.

"Of course. It is the driver of the saloon car."

We now knew a little more, but not enough to take the investigation much further. There was a reason why the car had turned

---

* A native spirit distilled from rice.

northwards, but it wasn't easy to figure out. A few miles beyond Puttalam the road entered the most formidable jungle country to be found in Ceylon—it was elephant territory and lonely and dangerous.

For two days we tried to get a bead on John Silva, but nowhere could we find a trace of him, nor were the fingerprints found in the abandoned car of any help to us. None of them matched those in our files. The police at Puttalam, however, received an anonymous postcard saying that Silva was hiding in the jungle with the money stolen from the Turf Club.

It was quite impossible to judge if this message was genuine or from a crackpot or some wretch who could not resist trying to hoax the police—an old trick known to every police officer.

Searching for someone in the Puttalam jungle was like looking for water in the Sahara, but it was, as far as I could see, the only move left on the board, as we got a party together. We split up into small groups and, by one of those freak chances, we got a lucky break.

Two of our searchers worked their way deep into the jungle and for a time were lost. Late in the afternoon, however, and when almost exhausted, they came across a narrow track which they recognised was a way out. They followed it along, and had not gone far when they came across the body of John Silva at a place about two hundred yards from the road.

It was a chilling sight. A gas mask covered the face of the dead man and he was tied to a tree. His legs, from the ankles to the knees, were trussed and his arms were drawn backwards and then roped upwards, so that his body, slightly bent and in a half-crouching position, provided a parody of crucifixion. Great coils of rope entwined his body and the trunk of the tree to which he was tied. He was fully clothed except for one shoe which lay close by.

The breathing tube of the gas mask had been blocked and death was due to asphyxia and shock. There were minor injuries to the face and hands, but it was the blocked gas mask that had hastened death.

"This fiendish arrangement killed Silva within half an hour," said the doctor who performed the post-mortem. "Even without it he was tied up in such a manner that he could not have survived longer than ten to twelve hours, perhaps even less."

We still did not know the identity of Silva's killers, but unquestionably they were the men in whose company he had been seen in Puttalam. The way in which he had been killed suggested that the ringleader was a person of monstrous cruelty and strong enough to impose his will on the others. The search for the hold-up gang had now become a murder hunt, and scores of people during the next few weeks were interrogated in Colombo and Puttalam. As many agents as could be spared spent their time in the oddest places listening to scraps of conversation that might betray the murderers, but it was no good. People talked about the crime, but not about the killers.

The break-through, however, as often happens, came from within, so to speak, and one day one of my detectives found a man who said he wanted to make a full confession. He was the driver of the Standard car that the owner of the eating-house in Puttalam had linked with the stolen car and its occupants. I gave the man a seat at my desk, where he sat trembling in the grip of shattered nerves.

"I cannot stand it any longer," he burst out. "The strain is too terrible and I feel it is destroying me. I watched them tie up Silva and force the tube of the gas mask into his mouth. The ropes held him so tightly he could not struggle. He just crouched there like a poor, stricken animal."

"Let us have the truth and from the very beginning," I said.

"If I turn King's evidence does it mean that I shall not be prosecuted?"

I reminded him that he had come of his own free will to confess and not to make a bargain "It does not rest with me but with the authorities," I said. "You are an accomplice, but it is possible that you may be dealt with more leniently by telling the truth under oath."

He nodded and then began:

"The robbery was planned some time ago, and for several weeks we watched the offices of the Turf Club every Monday morning. The routine, as we discovered, did not vary and it was possible to calculate, almost to a second, how long it took for the money to be carried out to the waiting car and then to the bank.

"We needed the car that was used every week, and the only way to get it was to hire it the day before, keep it overnight, and substitute our own men for the regular driver and police officer who always rode with him.

"On the Sunday before the robbery Silva was the only driver on duty at the garage and he drove the others to Puttalam. I followed with two of my friends in the Standard. At Puttalam, Silva was given plenty of arrack to drink so that he would not ask too many questions. After leaving the eating-house he was told to drive along the jungle road. I had gone on ahead for some little distance, but I pulled into the side and allowed the saloon to overtake me. After that I kept the saloon in sight.

"Thirteen miles beyond Puttalam one of the men in the saloon feigned illness, and Silva was ordered to stop the car. Everybody got out for a breath of air, so they said, and by then it was quite dark.

"I stopped the Standard not far away and my two friends got out and tied black handkerchiefs over their faces as a disguise. One had a revolver and the other carried a big coil of rope. It had been arranged what they should do and they crept up on the others. They told Silva to put his hands behind his back, and when he resisted he was punched in the face. To make the hold-up appear genuine Silva's passengers also had their hands tied and we all went into the jungle.

"Silva was then bound to the tree and a gas mask put over his face and we left him there. It was awful and I felt terribly sorry for him.

"We returned to Colombo that night and the way was now open for the robbery. Early next morning we telephoned the garage to say that the Turf Club wanted a car sent later than usual. Nobody, it seemed, had an inkling of the truth. For the rest, you know what happened."

Having unburdened himself the witness clasped his hands together and waited for me to speak. He knew quite well the question I was going to ask.

"I want the names of everybody implicated in the murder and robbery."

"If I tell you who these men are, and where they can be found, can I be given police protection until they are arrested?"

I nodded, and he gave me the names and addresses of eight

persons. The arrests were carried out by Superintendent Albert de Silva and Assistant Superintendent B. W. Perera.

At the preliminary hearing three of the prisoners were found not guilty and discharged. Among the remaining five committed for trial were an ex-policeman who had served in the Ceylon Garrison Artillery during the war, and was familiar with gas-mask drill, an ex-member of the Royal Army Service Corps in the Middle East, and a student of indigenous medicine.

It was pleaded on behalf of the accused that the death of Silva was not a premeditated act and that he had been tied up in the jungle to keep him out of the way until the hold-up had been accomplished. The anonymous postcard, said the defence, corroborated this view and had been sent to the police at Puttalam so that Silva might be discovered and released.

The court, however, rejected this explanation and four of the prisoners, M. Wijedasa Perera, M. A. L. Warlis Munasinghe, M. A. Don James Senivaratne and R. L. Premalal (alias J. P. Rajapakee, alias Vedemahatmaya) were found guilty and duly executed. The fifth escaped the death sentence but received a term of ten years' imprisonment.

About two-thirds of the stolen money— £ 27,000—was recovered from the homes of the accused, and with this discovery the official file on the case was closed. Altogether three years had gone by from the night John Silva was left to die in the jungle to the day when judgment was visited on his killers.

All that justice could achieve had been done, but there was, nevertheless, an aspect of the case that remained a mystery. The prosecution was never able to discover whose "brains" had inspired the robbery and the diabolical manner of Silva's death. The postcard was not, as had been so desperately urged in court, a message of mercy, but a black-edged notification by a killer that somewhere in the dark Puttalam jungle was to be found the body of a man who had died trying to breathe through a choked gas mask.

Crime Without Corpse

by Assistant Police Commissioner Alex Haslund, Chief of the C.I.D., Copenhagen, Denmark

LONG BEFORE half a bucketful of sludge betrayed John George Haigh, high priest of the acid bath, to the executioner, in fact in 1932, the body of a girl killed in Copenhagen disappeared into limbo. Not a solitary trace was ever found of her; neither tissue nor hair—not even the ashes of her incineration. Her body was cut up and burnt in a kitchen stove, as we found out after an exasperatingly tortuous investigation, and so incredible did it appear to us that a corpse could be disposed of in this way that we cremated a pig's head in just the same manner.

The experiment, and we recognised it was not without a lick of irreverence, merely confirmed what we had secretly feared—which was that if nothing can be wholly destroyed the last vestiges of a crime may well have disappeared before a detective knocks at the door of a suspect.

This is exactly what took place in the case that became known throughout Denmark as the "Elna Mystery" and which culminated in that strangest of all judicial paradoxes—a trial for murder without a corpse.

The girl who died was Elna, a vivacious nineteen-year-old brunette with a bright appetite for excitement she had never been able to satisfy either on Fanö, an island off the west coast of Jutland, where she was born, or in the provinces where she had worked as a servant. Her parents were fisherfolk and they had hoped that their daughter would marry the sailor to whom she had become engaged, but Elna had no desire to become just another little provincial housewife and she broke it off.

She liked men well enough, though, but on her own terms—in the taverns, cheap restaurants and dance halls she found in Copenhagen when she arrived there in 1932.

In the beginning she worked as a maid, but there was not enough time to play and she gave up her job and slept where she could, perhaps at the apartment of a girl friend or with some stray acquaintance she had picked up in a tavern or at the Tivoli, Copenhagen's pleasure park, which enchanted her.

One of Elna's favourite spots was a dance hall known as "The Chain." It was in the centre of the city and popular with shop girls, servants, seamen, white-collar workers and tarts and their pimps. It was here that she met the man by whose hand she was to die four months later.

Paul N. was fifty, divorced, and the father of a grown-up family. He was powerfully built and rugged and had spent many years at sea. He talked so well about the countries he had seen that women, especially young women like Elna, were fascinated by him. Superficially he was amusing and not ungenerous when it suited his purpose, but there was a sinister side to his nature. He was possessive, easily lost his temper, and in these moods became ugly and dangerous.

When Elna met him he had not been to sea for a long time. He had worked as a fireman and then as a chauffeur, but for the last few years he had lived on State assistance and the money he earned as an abortionist.

Elna found Paul irresistible and she had not known him long when she went to live with him in a two-room flat in a cluster of old houses in Christianshavn, one of the most ancient parts of Copenhagen. The house lay close to the old fortification dykes and had a small garden. Paul's rooms were well kept and filled with pictures and souvenirs of his voyages abroad.

Thus for the first time since she had given up her job Elna had a bed of her own, which, of course, she shared with her ardent lover. Paul was careful with his money and kept a record of his daily expenses, but so great was his infatuation for the fisherman's daughter that when she wanted to visit her parents in Fanö he paid for the holiday and bought her a new dress in blue, which was her favourite colour.

She had promised to return to him, but Paul was beset by the uncertainty that afflicts the jealous and he wrote constantly asking her to come back. In August Elna rejoined her middle-aged lover and sent a little note to her parents to say that she had arrived safely. That was the last they ever heard from her. They had, of course, no inkling that she was the mistress of a man old enough to be her father or the kind of life she was leading.

Early in October of the same year they got a letter from Paul saying that Elna had just left for England with a Mr. Owen. It was all he could tell them, he said, and he was unable to give them her address. As the months went by, and no word was received from the girl, her family became anxious, but it was not until the following April—that is, in 1933—they came to us with the story of their daughter's disappearance and asked us to try to trace her.

When we began to probe into the girl's brief history it soon became evident that she might well have left Paul for another man and gone abroad. But Mr. Owen, who Paul claimed was her new lover, was supposedly an Englishman. Elna, however, did not speak a word of English, perhaps no great impediment between lovers at play, but how did they make their plans to go away together? There must have been a third party, at least at the beginning, but only Paul, seemingly, had met Mr. Owen or knew of his existence.

The whisper got around in the taverns and dance halls that Paul had strangled Elna and destroyed her body and when it reached us we intensified our inquiries.

Paul, whom we had already questioned more than once, said he and Elna first met Owen at a dance hall. The Englishman was working at one of the stands at a British exhibition that had opened at the Tivoli and the girl had taken such a fancy to him that she had abandoned Paul and become his mistress. Owen bought her some new clothes and she left behind at Paul's place an old coat and a rust-coloured dress. According to Paul, Owen had taken Elna back with him to England on October 13th. He had received a card from his ex-mistress saying she was well and liked her new life, but she did not disclose where she was living.

We tried to find Mr. Owen, but my detectives established that no one of that name had been employed at the exhibition. We then checked every man named Owen who had visited Denmark in 1932. None of them came anywhere near Paul's description of the elusive Englishman. More significantly, Elna, if she had really left the country, had got out without the formality of a passport.

From friends and acquaintances of the missing girl we were able to take a closer look at her brief affair with Paul. It was a stormy attachment, for he hated to see her with another man and, one night at "The Chain," he had seized hold of her and begun to squeeze her throat. Elna became afraid of him.

Her closest friend was a girl named Jenny, whom we questioned. She told us that in September Elna left Paul and had gone to live with her because she could no longer stand his jealousy. Not long afterwards the two girls saw him at a dance and he pleaded with Elna to return and said that he would buy her a new hat as a peace offering.

Elna did not go back immediately, but the bait Paul had offered did the trick, and one day, when the girls were out together, Elna told her friend that she wanted the new hat and was going back to Paul. She left Jenny in the street and did not return that evening to the room they had shared together. Her friend never saw her again.

Some time later, Jenny told us, she went to see Paul to ask after Elna. He told her she was still living with him and had got a job in a restaurant. The next time she saw him he said that Elna had gone to England with a friend. Jenny was more than mildly astonished. Not only had Elna not come to say goodbye to her—an odd lapse between affectionate friends—but she had left her clothes and trinkets behind. It was so unlike Elna to behave in this strange way!

A full portrait of Paul provided an unsavoury picture. He was hot-tempered and jealous and had treated his ex-wife brutally. After his divorce many young girls visited his flat and he had become known as an abortionist under the name of "Doctor N."

Although we were convinced that Elna was no longer alive, and that Paul could explain her disappearance if he cared to, we had not the necessary proof to charge him with murder. We wanted him, though, and in June 1933 he was arrested on various counts of carrying out illegal operations.

He admitted he was an abortionist when he realised that we had plenty of evidence to convict him, but he would not deviate from

his original explanation of the disappearance of Elna, even though
we reminded him that nobody, excepting himself, had ever seen
the girl in the company of the mysterious Mr. Owen. When we said
how inexplicable it was that she should suddenly break with her
friend Jenny and stop writing to her parents, with whom she had
never before failed to keep in touch, Paul shrugged his shoulders
and with a sly smile said that the girl was her own master and he
could not be held responsible for the way she acted.

We knew he was lying, but he was so assured and bland that it
was obvious that something quite out of the blue was required to
wrest the truth from him. Everything that was humanly possible
had been done to find the body of the missing girl. Paul's garden,
and those of his neighbours, had been dug up and canals and even
the port itself had been dragged in the search. Even the man with
the divining-rod turned up—certain that the body could be found
within the length of a barren coastal strip outside the capital!

But, quite literally, something out of the blue did emerge as a
result of the patient and systematic work of the detectives engaged
on the case. Among the papers in Paul's flat we discovered a cash
receipt from one of the big stores in the city. It was for the blue
summer dress Paul had bought Elna for her holiday at Fanö. The
dress was not among the clothes left with Jenny nor was it to be
found in the flat. Throughout Paul had denied that he had sold or
given away any clothes belonging to Elna, and our inquiries convinced us that the blue dress had not been sold, whatever had
happened to it. Paul, we knew, had a frugal mind. He had never
been prodigal, either with his money or possessions, and it was
most unlikely that he had destroyed the dress. There could be only
one explanation. He had given it to one of his new girl friends!

This was plumb-line reckoning, and, difficult as it was to get any
of Paul's friends to provide us with information, we found at last
a young girl to whom he had made a gift of the dress in the autumn
of 1932. Some little time before his arrest he had gone to see her
and told her to burn the dress. She had been too frightened not to
obey or to tell the police.

We asked Paul if he had ever given Elna a blue dress. Yes, he
had, and he was sure she had taken it with her to England. He was
obviously very confident that it had been destroyed. The dress, we
learned, was a model and only three of its kind had been made and

sold, but the store remembered it from the description we were able to give them and an exact replica was made for us, even to the quality and texture of the material.

Paul by now had been in custody for several months, ostensibly for his crimes as an abortionist, but he was much less cocksure than when he was first arrested. We now had something tangible to question him about, in fact we possessed some damning "evidence"—the blue dress itself, or something deceptively like it.

The police interrogator decided that the time was opportune for a confession, and he again began to question Paul about Elna's clothes. Had he sold any of them or given any away?

Paul said "No" to both questions and the interrogator then led him to an adjoining room where the blue dress lay on a table.

"Do you recognise this dress?" he was asked.

Paul stood motionless and silent staring at something he had believed no longer existed. "Yes," he said quietly, "I killed Elna. I will tell you all about it."

I have heard confessions burst out in great cataracts of emotion, but not that of Paul's. It was cool and detached as if he were speaking of somebody other than himself—somebody of whom he was prepared to concede undoubted cleverness; but the act itself, the dismemberment, the incineration, and the reason for everything—they simply nurtured his innate cynicism.

He said that Elna feared pregnancy, and that at her prompting he began an operation on her to bring about sterility. It was never completed because, quite accidentally, he perforated her womb and the girl lost consciousness and died within three hours. Paul said he became frightened and decided to burn the body.

The following day he cut it up with a bread-knife and hacksaw and wrapped the various parts in newspapers and stacked them underneath the kitchen table. For the next five days he burned them one by one in the kitchen stove. Alley cats, attracted by the smell, gathered in the garden and he threw them the heart, lungs and liver. He expected, said Paul, that the neighbours would complain of the unbearable smell—and he himself had to smoke continuously—but nobody said a word. When the final parcel was disposed of he removed the last of the ashes to the dustbin and that was all that remained of the body. Paul explained that he had only one visitor during the five days he was busy with Elna's remains, a young girl whom he got rid of by telling her he had a "patient" to whom he was attending.

We were sceptical about the entire confession. Elna was too carefree to worry about possible pregnancy and the story of her desiring to be made sterile appeared too tall to be true. Paul was persuaded to repeat his explanation of her death in the presence of a doctor from the department of forensic medicine at Copenhagen University. He was closely questioned about the operation he said he had performed, but it was not possible to discover any inconsistencies in his story of the girl's death.

We searched the kitchen stove and chimney, but found nothing. To test Paul's claim that he had even burnt the girl's head in the same way as he had other parts of the body, we "cremated" a pig's head. It, too, was reduced to mere ashes.

Paul N., nevertheless, stood trial for murder in February 1954, but a jury found him not guilty of intentionally murdering Elna. For "unintentionally killing her under aggravating circumstances," and for his offences as an abortionist, he received a sentence of five years' imprisonment.

A Rope for Margarita

by Police Commissar Gregory Arensky,
Moscow, U.S.S.R.

O NE COULD not tell what twenty-two-year-old Margarita Lapina Tikhomirov had looked like. When I saw her she was hanging from a beam, her tongue thrust out, her face suffused by broken blood vessels and her eyes protruding from their sockets and glazed like smoked glass.

I heard someone say among the excited throng in the Tikhomirov apartment at Kirova U 1, Krasnodtyabrsky (Moscow's Red October Street) that she had been a pretty girl and a devoted wife to Georgi Tikhomirov, the sweetheart of her childhood. It was a great pity, everybody said, that such a fine girl should take her own life so cruelly and painfully. Of course, if only somebody had been in the apartment that evening when she had returned from work they could have calmed her. But no one was there and she had tied a rope to the beam, put a noose over her head and jumped off the chair that lay overturned near the body. How unlucky it was that Margarita's husband was working late and that his parents Valentina Semyonovna and Nikolas Tikhomirov were also absent.

It was the girl's mother-in-law, returning from a walk, who had found the body and whose agonised cries had brought the family's neighbours running to the apartment. "I knew she would lay hands on herself," cried Valentina, "I could see she was losing her mind."

Two neighbours held the body while one of my detectives, Anatoly Bezuglov, untied the knot that had secured the rope to the beam and handed me the rope with the noose still intact. We got the body on to a bed and I could see there was some bruising round the lips. I slipped the noose over the face of the dead girl and Bezuglov helped me turn the body over. He looked at me sharply at something he, too, noticed and I whispered to him to get rid of the spectators while I examined the apartment. In a corner of the kitchen, near a heater, I picked up a couple of glasses, wrapped them in a handkerchief and slipped them into my pocket.

Just as the ambulance-hearse was about to leave with the body, Georgi Tikhomirov, the husband of the dead girl, burst into the room. He was wild with grief and as he pulled the sheet away, and looked at the distorted face of the wife he had long loved, he began to sob. He looked very ill and at the end of his strength.

It was nearly midnight when Bezuglov and I left. The snow lay thinly on the broad pavements outside and sparkled like powdered diamonds under the street lights. Bezuglov put up the collar of his coat and, with a glance at the apartment building, said, "A little odd, isn't it, that everybody was conveniently out when the girl came home to kill herself?"

"Yes, very odd. I wonder how she got those bruises round her mouth? They looked to me to have been caused by violence—as if a hand had been put over her mouth to keep her quiet. I don't like the look of this case. We shall have to find out what kind of people these Tikhomirovs are and how they treated their daughter-in-law."

From neighbours and friends we gradually got together, so to speak, a family portrait. Margarita, the dead girl, was a war orphan and her only brother was killed at Stalingrad. The Government paid for her education and, from the age of seven, she had various foster-parents until her mother's sister gave her a home without showing her much affection.

Margarita was fourteen when she met Georgi Tikhomirov who was two years older. They became sweethearts and, as ardent children of the Soviet, they wandered together into science museums and art galleries, held hands at the theatre and cinema, and swore to each other that they would never be parted. When Georgi was eighteen, they promised themselves, they would get married.

Valentina, Georgi's mother, had, however, other plans for her son. She chose a girl for him who would bring him a dowry and whose family would help him. "You must forget that little orphan," she said. "She hasn't a kopek to her name and you will never have a home of your own if you do not marry a girl with money."

Georgi's father, Nikolas, looked with admiration at his wife. She knew what was best for her son and, indeed, for all the family. Her word was law. Nevertheless Georgi and Margarita were married secretly and Valentina took them in, her heart filled with hatred against her pretty daughter-in-law.

Valentina's sharp tongue wagged unceasingly and maliciously and although Georgi tried to pacify her she would not leave Margarita alone. The young couple tried to find a room elsewhere, but had no luck and Margarita, afraid that Georgi, who had once been in a sanatorium, might become ill again, persuaded him to give up his job in a brick works and take a course at an academy as an engraver. She herself attended classes for instruction in midwifery.

In 1952 the young couple were as poor as ever and Margarita wrote to her aunt in Tiflis saying:

"We have neither sufficient clothing nor enough food and Georgi needs a lot of care if he is not to become tubercular again. His mother is terribly difficult and would skin you alive for a piece of bread. She brags about the ten thousand rubles she has saved from the embroidery she sells, but we want nothing from her and I would be happy if only she would cease abusing me."

As if the situation was not bad enough already, Margarita gave birth to a son. It was a happy event for everybody excepting Valentina. Even Nikolas, weak and under her domination, loved his grandchild, but Valentina would not look at the baby.

Four months after it was born it was supposedly choked by a rubber teether. Margarita and Georgi were out at the time and so, too, were the grandparents, according to the police. The child's death was accepted as an unfortunate accident for which nobody was culpable.

Georgi, recalling the death of his son, told me that on the day of the funeral his mother stood near the little coffin eating an ice-cream. So callously did she behave that he was struck by a terrible thought.

We found out that for some time before Margarita's death Valentina had been telling everyone that her daughter-in-law was insane and might commit suicide at any time. One of the glasses I had taken away from the Tikhomirov apartment bore fingerprints that did not belong to any of the family and I found a neighbour who told me that on the night of the tragedy he had seen Valentina enter her apartment with a woman he did not know. Within a week I had traced this very woman to Khovrino where she lived. Her name was Vera Rybakova. She was an old friend of Valentina and it was her hand that had left the fingerprints on the glass.

I now knew what lay behind the death of Margarita and, towards the end of May 1956, the trial began in Moscow of Valentina and Nikolas Tikhomirov and Vera Rybakova for the murder of the young wife.

It was possible to show that for two years Valentina had planned to murder her daughter-in-law. She had first to convince Nikolas that Georgi could be "saved" only by getting rid of his wife. Nikolas yielded eventually, but insisted that they must have somebody to do the job. Valentina did not know to whom she could turn, but one day over a drink with Medvedyeva, one of her cronies who bought all the embroidery she made, Valentina was told, "You know, Vera Rybakova is a good one. She's gone through plenty in her time and she can be relied upon."

Valentina sent to Khovrino for Vera and the pair quickly came to terms. Perhaps for the only time in her life Valentina did not try to bargain, but made a straight offer.

"Five thousand rubles when the job is done and you also get the trophies of the chase," she said, indicating that Vera could take away everything belonging to the intended victim.

They fixed a night when Georgi was working late at his job and when they knew that Margarita would be home long before her husband. So that Georgi could get the food and medicine he needed, Margarita went out nursing and was due back that evening about nine o'clock. Valentina collected Vera and returned to the apartment with her. The women found Nikolas apprehensive and short of courage, but Valentina got out a bottle of vodka and it helped to steady their nerves.

When Margarita opened the apartment door Valentina and Vera hid behind the curtains and, as they had arranged, Nikolas went into the little kitchen and called out, "Come and have a glass of tea, Margarita. You must be very tired after your long day."

The girl may have become suspicious over this sudden concern Nikolas was showing for her or she may, indeed, have been too weary even to reply. The conspirators waited, puzzled by the girl's silence, but slowly, and it seemed uncertainly, she walked into the kitchen. As she did so Rybakova stole out of her hiding place and sneaked up behind the girl. She had a rope in her hands and slipped a noose over the girl's head and began to pull. Margarita managed to break free, but Nikolas intercepted her dash to the door and she pleaded with him.

"Father dear," she said, "let me go. I promise I shall not say a word of this to anyone."

Tikhomirov did not answer, but thrust his hand over the girl's mouth to prevent her screaming. Vera Rybakova pulled the noose tight and in a few minutes the victim had been strangled and her body hoisted up to the beam. A chair was tipped over and it set the stage for Margarita's "suicide."

In the early stages of the trial the accused denied that there had been a conspiracy or that they had killed Margarita. The court asked for my testimony and I said:

"Margarita Tikhomirov did not take her own life. She was murdered. The knot of the noose would have broken her neck had she jumped from a chair. The abrasions on the neck were not at the back, but at the side, where the noose had been pulled taut."

This theory was confirmed by medical experts.

There were many witnesses to testify to Valentina's hatred of the dead girl and how persistently she had suggested to neighbours that Margarita was becoming insane, but the most damning piece of evidence was the proof that Valentina's companion on the night of the murder was Vera Rybakova.

It was the woman from Khovrino who was the first to wilt under the strain of the trial. She admitted she was in the apartment and poured herself a drink of vodka after "watching" the crime being committed.

Valentina, livid with rage, turned on Rybakova. She said that the five thousand rubles in Vera's possession showed who was the real murderess. These and other accusations, which the two women flung at each other in an attempt to save themselves, made it perfectly clear that both of them and Nikolas Tikhomirov were guilty.

The public prosecutor, Mr. Rosakov, in his closing address to the court had a sharp word to say about the attitude of neighbours of the Tikhomirovs. Without exception they had admitted they knew how badly Margarita was treated. They had not interfered, they had said in their testimony, because they felt it was solely a family matter. The prosecutor believed otherwise.

"Not one of these witnesses," he pointed out, "had the courage to say, 'This can't go on. The Tikhomirovs are not treating their daughter-in-law fairly and have put themselves beyond the pale of decent men and women.'

"If the neighbours had ostracised the Tikhomirovs from the very beginning this murder would not have taken place. Instead, they passively accepted a situation that was intolerable. Nobody is justified in closing their eyes to cruelty, merely by proclaiming that family affairs are sacrosanct. Cruelty is everybody's concern, wherever it occurs."

The court was crowded to hear the verdict. In a dry, crisp voice the judge called for the attention of the accused and said that the charge of wilful murder having been examined, the court now found each of the accused guilty and sentenced them to be shot.

Georgi Tikhomirov did not look at his parents as they were led away together with Vera Rybakova. He had not displayed any emotion on hearing the sentence, but when the judge had withdrawn, Georgi got up, and avoiding those who still remained, walked away without speaking to anyone.